CHAPTERS ON
JEWISH LITERATURE

ISRAEL ABRAHAMS
Author of "Jewish Life in the Middle Ages"

CHAPTERS ON
JEWISH LITERATURE

BIBLIOBAZAAR

CHAPTERS ON
JEWISH LITERATURE

PREFACE

These twenty-five short chapters on Jewish Literature open with the fall of Jerusalem in the year 70 of the current era, and end with the death of Moses Mendelssohn in 1786. Thus the period covered extends over more than seventeen centuries. Yet, long as this period is, it is too brief. To do justice to the literature of Judaism even in outline, it is clearly necessary to include the Bible, the Apocrypha, and the writings of Alexandrian Jews, such as Philo. Only by such an inclusion can the genius of the Hebrew people be traced from its early manifestations through its inspired prime to its brilliant after-glow in the centuries with which this little volume deals.

One special reason has induced me to limit this book to the scope indicated above. The Bible has been treated in England and America in a variety of excellent text-books written by and for Jews and Jewesses. It seemed to me very doubtful whether the time is, or ever will be, ripe for dealing with the Scriptures from the purely literary stand-point in teaching young students. But this is the stand-point of this volume. Thus I have refrained from including the Bible, because, on the one hand, I felt that I could not deal with it as I have tried to deal with the rest of Hebrew literature, and because, on the other hand, there was no necessity for me to attempt to add to the books already in use. The sections to which I have restricted myself are only rarely taught to young students in a consecutive manner, except in so far as they fall within the range of lessons on Jewish History. It was strongly urged on me by a friend of great experience and knowledge, that a small text-book on later Jewish Literature was likely to be found useful both for home and school use. Such a book might encourage the elementary study of Jewish literature in a wider circle than has hitherto been reached. Hence this book has been compiled with the definite aim of providing an elementary manual. It will be seen that both in the inclusions and exclusions the author has followed a line of his own, but he lays no claim to originality. The book is simply designed as a manual for those who may wish to master some of the leading characteristics of the subject, without burdening themselves with too many details and dates.

This consideration has in part determined also the method of the book. In presenting an outline of Jewish literature three plans are possible. One can divide the subject according to *Periods*. Starting with the Rabbinic Age and closing with the activity of the earlier Gaonim, or Persian Rabbis, the First Period would carry us to the eighth or the ninth century. A well-marked Second Period is that of the Arabic-Spanish writers, a period which would extend from the ninth to the fifteenth century. From the sixteenth to the eighteenth century forms a Third Period with distinct characteristics. Finally, the career of Mendelssohn marks the definite beginning of the Modern Period. Such a grouping of the facts presents many advantages, but it somewhat obscures the varying conditions prevalent at one and the same time in different countries where the Jews were settled. Hence some writers have preferred to arrange the material under the different *Countries*. It is quite possible to draw a map of the world's civilization by merely marking the successive places in which Jewish literature has fixed its head-quarters. But, on the other hand, such a method of classification has the disadvantage that it leads to much overlapping. For long intervals together, it is impossible to separate Italy from Spain, France from Germany, Persia from Egypt, Constantinople from Amsterdam. This has induced other writers to propose a third method and to trace *Influences*, to indicate that, whereas Rabbinism may be termed the native product of the Jewish genius, the scientific, poetical, and philosophical tendencies of Jewish writers in the Middle Ages were due to the interaction of external and internal forces. Further, in this arrangement, the Ghetto period would have a place assigned to it as such, for it would again mark the almost complete sway of purely Jewish forces in Jewish literature. Adopting this classification, we should have a wave of Jewish impulse, swollen by the accretion of foreign waters, once more breaking on a Jewish strand, with its contents in something like the same condition in which they left the original spring. All these three methods are true, and this has impelled me to refuse to follow any one of them to the exclusion of the other two. I have tried to trace *influences*, to observe *periods*, to distinguish *countries*. I have also tried to derive color and vividness by selecting prominent personalities round which to group whole cycles of facts. Thus, some of the chapters bear the names of famous men, others are entitled from periods, others from countries, and yet others are named from the general currents of European thought. In all this my aim has been very modest. I have done little in the way of literary criticism, but I felt that a dry collection of names and dates was the very thing I had to avoid. I need not say that I have done my best to ensure accuracy in my statements by referring to the best authorities known to me on each division of the subject. To name the works to which I am indebted would need a list of many of the best-known products of recent Continental and American scholarship. At the end of every chapter I have, however, given references to some English works and essays. Graetz is cited in the English translation published by the Jewish Publication Society of America. The figures in brackets refer to the edition published in London. The American and the English editions of S. Schechter's "Studies in Judaism" are similarly referred to.

Of one thing I am confident. No presentation of the facts, however bald and inadequate it be, can obscure the truth that this little book deals with a great and an inspiring literature. It is possible to question whether the books of great Jews always belonged to the great books of the world. There may have been, and there were, greater legalists than Rashi, greater poets than Jehuda Halevi, greater philosophers than Maimonides, greater moralists than Bachya. But there has been no greater literature than that which these and numerous other Jews represent.

Rabbinism was a sequel to the Bible, and if like all sequels it was unequal to its original, it nevertheless shared its greatness. The works of all Jews up to the modern period were the sequel to this sequel. Through them all may be detected the unifying principle that literature in its truest sense includes life itself; that intellect is the handmaid to conscience; and that the best books are those which best teach men how to live. This underlying unity gave more harmony to Jewish literature than is possessed by many literatures more distinctively national. The maxim, "Righteousness delivers from death," applies to books as well as to men. A literature whose consistent theme is Righteousness is immortal. On the very day on which Jerusalem fell, this theory of the interconnection between literature and life became the fixed principle of Jewish thought, and it ceased to hold undisputed sway only in the age of Mendelssohn. It was in the "Vineyard" of Jamnia that the theory received its firm foundation. A starting-point for this volume will therefore be sought in the meeting-place in which the Rabbis, exiled from the Holy City, found a new fatherland in the Book of books.

CONTENTS

CHAPTER I

THE "VINEYARD" AT JAMNIA

Schools at Jamnia, Lydda, Usha, and Sepphoris.—The Tannaim compile the Mishnah.—Jochanan, Akiba, Meir, Judah.—Aquila.

The story of Jewish literature, after the destruction of the Temple at Jerusalem in the year 70 of the Christian era, centres round the city of Jamnia. Jamnia, or Jabneh, lay near the sea, beautifully situated on the slopes of a gentle hill in the lowlands, about twenty-eight miles from the capital. When Vespasian was advancing to the siege of Jerusalem, he occupied Jamnia, and thither the Jewish Synhedrion, or Great Council, transferred itself when Jerusalem fell. A college existed there already, but Jamnia then became the head-quarters of Jewish learning, and retained that position till the year 135. At that date the learned circle moved further north, to Galilee, and, besides the famous school at Lydda in Judea, others were founded in Tiberias, Usha, and Sepphoris.

The real founder of the College at Jamnia was Jochanan, the son of Zakkai, called "the father of wisdom." Like the Greek philosophers who taught their pupils in the gardens of the "Academy" at Athens, the Rabbis may have lectured to their students in a "Vineyard" at Jamnia. Possibly the term "Vineyard" was only a metaphor applied to the meeting-place of the Wise at Jamnia, but, at all events, the result of these pleasant intellectual gatherings was the Rabbinical literature. Jochanan himself was a typical Rabbi. For a great part of his life he followed a mercantile pursuit, and earned his bread by manual labor. His originality as a teacher lay in his perception that Judaism could survive the loss of its national centre. He felt that "charity and the love of men may replace the sacrifices." He would have preferred his brethren to submit to Rome, and his political foresight was justified when the war of independence closed in disaster. As Graetz has well said, like Jeremiah Jochanan wept over the desolation of Zion, but like Zerubbabel he created a new sanctuary. Jochanan's new sanctuary was the school.

In the "Vineyard" at Jamnia, the Jewish tradition was the subject of much animated inquiry. The religious, ethical, and practical literature of the past was sifted and treasured, and fresh additions were made. But not much was written, for until the close of the second century the new literature of the Jews was *oral*. The Bible was written down, and read from scrolls, but the Rabbinical literature was committed to memory piecemeal, and handed down from teacher to pupil. Notes were perhaps taken in writing, but even when the Oral Literature was collected, and arranged as a book, it is believed by many authorities that the book so compiled remained for a considerable period an oral and not a written book.

This book was called the *Mishnah* (from the verb *shana*, "to repeat" or "to learn"). The Mishnah was not the work of one man or of one age. So long was it in growing, that its birth dates from long before the destruction of the Temple. But the men most closely associated with the compilation of the Mishnah were the Tannaim (from the root *tana*, which has the same meaning as *shana*). There were about one hundred and twenty of these Tannaim between the years 70 and 200 C.E., and they may be conveniently arranged in four generations. From each generation one typical representative will here be selected.

THE TANNAIM

First Generation, 70 to 100 C.E.
JOCHANAN, the son of Zakkai

Second Generation, 100 to 130 C.E.
AKIBA

Third Generation, 130 to 160 C.E.

MEIR

Fourth Generation, 160 to 200 C.E.

JUDAH THE PRINCE

The Tannaim were the possessors of what was perhaps the greatest principle that dominated a literature until the close of the eighteenth century. They maintained that *literature* and *life* were co-extensive. It was said of Jochanan, the son of Zakkai, that he never walked a single step without thinking of God. Learning the Torah, that is, the Law, the authorized Word of God, and its Prophetical and Rabbinical developments, was man's supreme duty. "If thou hast learned much Torah, ascribe not any merit to thyself, for therefor wast thou created." Man was created to learn; literature was the aim of life. We have already seen what kind of literature. Jochanan once said to his five favorite disciples: "Go forth and consider which is the good way to which a man should cleave." He received various answers, but he most approved of this response: "A good heart is the way." Literature is life if it be a heart-literature—this may be regarded as the final justification of the union effected in the Mishnah between learning and righteousness.

Akiba, who may be taken to represent the second generation of Tannaim, differed in character from Jochanan. Jochanan had been a member of the peace party in the years 66 to 70; Akiba was a patriot, and took a personal part in the later struggle against Rome, which was organized by the heroic Bar Cochba in the years 131 to 135. Akiba set his face against frivolity, and pronounced silence a fence about wisdom. But his disposition was resolute rather than severe. Of him the most romantic of love stories is told. He was a herdsman, and fell in love with his master's daughter, who endured poverty as his devoted wife, and was glorified in her husband's fame. But whatever contrast there may have been in the two characters, Akiba, like Jochanan, believed that a literature was worthless unless it expressed itself in the life of the scholar. He and his school held in low esteem the man who, though learned, led an evil life, but they took as their ideal the man whose moral excellence was more conspicuous than his learning. As R. Eleazar, the son of Azariah, said: "He whose knowledge is in excess of his good deeds is like a tree whose branches are many and its roots scanty; the wind comes, uproots, and overturns it. But he whose good deeds are more than his knowledge is like a tree with few branches but many roots, so that if all the winds in the world come and blow upon it, it remains firm in its place." Man, according to Akiba, is master of his own destiny; he needs God's grace to triumph over evil, yet the triumph depends on his own efforts: "Everything is seen, yet freedom of choice is given; the world is judged by grace, yet all is according to the work." The Torah, the literature of Israel, was to Akiba "a desirable instrument," a means to life.

Among the distinctions of Akiba's school must be named the first literal translation of the Bible into Greek. This work was done towards the close of the second century by Aquila, a proselyte, who was inspired by Akiba's teaching. Aquila's version was inferior to the Alexandrian Greek version, called the Septuagint, in graces of style, but was superior in accuracy. Aquila followed the Hebrew text word by word. This translator is identical with Onkelos, to whom in later centuries the Aramaic translation (*Targum* Onkelos) of the Pentateuch was ascribed. Aramaic versions of the Bible were made at a very early period, and the Targum Onkelos may contain ancient elements, but in its present form it is not earlier than the fifth century.

Meir, whom we take as representative of the third generation of Tannaim, was filled with the widest sympathies. In his conception of truth, everything that men can know belonged to the Torah. Not that the Torah superseded or absorbed all other knowledge, but that the Torah needed, for its right study, all the aids which science and secular information could supply. In this way Jewish literature was to some extent saved from the danger of becoming a merely religious exercise, and in later centuries, when the mass of Jews were disposed to despise and even discourage scientific and philosophical culture, a minority was always prepared to resist this tendency and, on the ground of the views of some of the Tannaim like Meir, claimed the right to study what we should now term secular sciences. The width of Meir's sympathies may be seen in his tolerant conduct towards his friend Elisha, the son of Abuya. When the latter forsook Judaism, Meir remained true to Elisha. He devoted himself to the effort to win back his old friend, and, though he failed, he never ceased to love him. Again, Meir was famed for his knowledge of fables, in antiquity a branch of the wisdom of all the Eastern world. Meir's large-mindedness was matched by his large-heartedness, and in his wife Beruriah he possessed a companion whose tender sympathies and fine toleration matched his own.

The fourth generation of Tannaim is overshadowed by the fame of Judah the Prince, *Rabbi*, as he was simply called. He lived from 150 to 210, and with his name is associated the compilation of the Mishnah. A man of genial manners, strong intellectual grasp, he was the exemplar also of princely hospitality and of friendship with others than Jews. His intercourse with one of the Antonines was typical of his wide culture. Life was not, in Rabbi Judah's view, compounded of smaller and larger incidents, but all the affairs of life were parts of the great divine scheme. "Reflect upon three things, and thou wilt not fall into the power of sin: Know what is above thee—a seeing eye and a hearing ear—and all thy deeds are written in a book."

The Mishnah, which deals with things great and small, with everything that concerns men, is the literary expression of this view of life. Its language is the new-Hebrew, a simple, nervous idiom suited to practical life, but lacking the power and poetry of the Biblical Hebrew. It is a more useful but less polished instrument than the older language. The subject-matter of the Mishnah includes both law and morality, the affairs of the body, of the soul, and of the mind. Business, religion, social duties, ritual, are all dealt with in one and the same code. The fault of this conception is, that by associating things of unequal importance, both the mind and the conscience may become incapable of discriminating the great from the small, the external from the spiritual. Another ill consequence was that, as literature corresponded so closely with life, literature could not correct the faults of life, when life became cramped or stagnant. The modern spirit differs from the ancient chiefly in that literature has now become an independent force, which may freshen and stimulate life. But the older ideal was nevertheless a great one. That man's life is a unity; that his conduct is in all its parts within the sphere of ethics and religion; that his mind and conscience are not independent, but two sides of the same thing; and that therefore his religious, ethical, æsthetic, and intellectual literature is one and indivisible,—this was a noble conception which, with all its weakness, had distinct points of superiority over the modern view.

The Mishnah is divided into six parts, or Orders (*Sedarim*); each Order into Tractates (*Massechtoth*); each Tractate into Chapters (*Perakim*); each Chapter into Paragraphs (each called a *Mishnah*). The six Orders are as follows:

ZERAIM ("Seeds"). Deals with the laws connected with Agriculture, and opens with a Tractate on Prayer ("Blessings").

MOED ("Festival"). On Festivals.

NASHIM ("Women"). On the laws relating to Marriage, etc.

NEZIKIN ("Damages"). On civil and criminal Law.

KODASHIM ("Holy Things"). On Sacrifices, etc.

TEHAROTH ("Purifications"). On personal and ritual Purity.

* * * * *

BIBLIOGRAPHY

THE MISHNAH.

> Graetz.—*History of the Jews*, English translation, Vol. II, chapters 13-17 (character of the Mishnah, end of ch. 17).
>
> Steinschneider.—*Jewish Literature* (London, 1857), p. 13.
>
> Schiller-Szinessy.—*Encyclopedia Britannica* (Ninth Edition), Vol. XVI, p. 502.
>
> De Sola and Raphall.—*Eighteen Tractates from the Mishnah* (English translation, London).
>
> C. Taylor.—*Sayings of the Jewish Fathers* (Cambridge, 1897).
>
> A. Kohut.—*The Ethics of the Fathers* (New York, 1885).
>
> G. Karpeles.—*A Sketch of Jewish History* (Jewish Publication Society of America, 1895), p. 40.

AQUILA.

> F.C. Burkitt.—*Jewish Quarterly Review*, Vol. X, p. 207.

CHAPTER II

FLAVIUS JOSEPHUS AND THE
JEWISH SIBYL

Great national crises usually produce an historical literature. This is more likely to happen with the nation that wins in a war than with the nation that loses. Thus, in the Maccabean period, historical works dealing with the glorious struggle and its triumphant termination were written by Jews both in Hebrew and in Greek. After the terrible misfortune which befell the Jews in the year 70, when Jerusalem sank before the Roman arms never to rise again, little heart was there for writing history. Jews sought solace in their existing literature rather than in new productions, and the Bible and the oral traditions that were to crystallize a century later into the Mishnah filled the national heart and mind. Yet more than one Jew felt an impulse to write the history of the dismal time. Thus the first complete books which appeared in Jewish literature after the loss of nationality were historical works written by two men, Justus and Josephus, both of whom bore an active part in the most recent of the wars which they recorded. Justus of Tiberias wrote in Greek a terse chronicle entitled, "History of the Jewish Kings," and also a more detailed narrative of the "Jewish War" with Rome. Both these books are known to us only from quotations. The originals are entirely lost. A happier fate has preserved the works of another Jewish historian of the same period, Flavius Josephus (38 to 95 C.E.), the literary and political opponent of Justus. He wrote three histories: "Antiquities of the Jews"; an "Autobiography"; "The Wars of the Jews"; together with a reply to the attacks of an Alexandrian critic of Judaism, "Against Apion." The character of Josephus has been variously estimated. Some regard him as a patriot, who yielded to Rome only when convinced that Jewish destiny required such submission. But the most probable view of his career is as follows. Josephus was a man of taste and learning. He was a student of the Greek and Latin classics, which he much admired, and was also a devoted and loyal lover of Judaism. Unfortunately, circumstances thrust him into a political position from which he could extricate himself only by treachery and duplicity. As a young man he had visited Rome, and there acquired enthusiastic admiration for the Romans. When he returned to Palestine, he found his countrymen filled with fiery patriotism and about to hurl themselves against the legions of the Caesars. To his dismay Josephus saw himself drawn into the patriotic vortex. By a strange mishap an important command was entrusted to him. He betrayed his country, and saved himself by eager submission to the Romans. He became a personal friend of Vespasian and the constant companion of his son Titus.

Traitor though he was to the national cause, Josephus was a steadfast champion of the Jewish religion. All his works are animated with a desire to present Judaism and the Jews in the best light. He was indignant that heathen historians wrote with scorn of the vanquished Jews, and resolved to describe the noble stand made by the Jewish armies against Rome. He was moved to wrath by the Egyptian Manetho's distortion of the ancient history of Israel, and he could not rest silent under the insults of Apion. The works of Josephus are therefore works written with a *tendency* to glorify his people and his religion. But they are in the main trustworthy, and are, indeed, one of the chief sources of information for the history of the Jews in post-Biblical times. His style is clear and attractive, and his power of grasping the events of long periods is comparable with that of Polybius. He was no mere chronicler; he possessed some faculty for explaining as well as recording facts and some real insight into the meaning of events passing under his own eyes.

He wrote for the most part in Greek, both because that language was familiar to many cultured Jews of his day, and because his histories thereby became accessible to the world of non-Jewish readers. Sometimes he used both Aramaic and Greek. For instance, he produced his "Jewish War" first in the one, subsequently in the other of these languages. The Aramaic version has been lost, but the Greek has survived. His style is often eloquent, especially in his book "Against Apion." This was an historical and philosophical justification of Judaism. At the close of this work Josephus says: "And so I make bold to say that we are become the teachers of other men in the greatest number of things, and those the most excellent." Josephus, like the Jewish Hellenists of an earlier date, saw in Judaism a universal religion, which ought to be shared by all the peoples of the earth. Judaism was to Josephus, as to Philo, not a contrast or antithesis to Greek culture, but the perfection and culmination of culture. *It was always universal and has n[...] to do c[...]*

The most curious efforts to propagate Judaism were, *Hell[...]* however, those which were clothed in a Sibylline disguise. In heathen antiquity, the Sibyl was an inspired prophetess whose mysterious oracles concerned the destinies of cities and nations. These oracles enjoyed high esteem among the cultivated Greeks, and, in the second century B.C.E., some Alexandrian Jews made use of them to recommend Judaism to the heathen world. In the Jewish Sibylline books the religion of Israel is presented as a hope and a threat; a menace to those who refuse to follow the better life, a promise of salvation to those who repent. About the year 80 C.E., a book of this kind was composed. It is what is known as the Fourth Book of the Sibylline Oracles. The language is Greek, the form hexameter verse. In this poem, the Sibyl, in the guise of a prophetess, tells of the doom of those who resist the will of the one true God, praises the God of Israel, and holds out a beautiful prospect to the faithful.

The book opens with an invocation:

> Hear, people of proud Asia, Europe, too,
> How many things by great, loud-sounding mouth,
> All true and of my own, I prophesy.
> No oracle of false Apollo this,
> Whom vain men call a god, tho' he deceived;
> But of the mighty God, whom human hands
> Shaped not like speechless idols cut in stone.

The Sibyl speaks of the true God, to love whom brings blessing. The ungodly triumph for a while, as Assyria, Media, Phrygia, Greece, and Egypt had triumphed. Jerusalem will fall, and the Temple perish in flames, but retribution will follow, the earth will be desolated by the divine wrath, the race of men and cities and rivers will be reduced to smoky dust, unless moral amendment comes betimes. Then the Sibyl's note changes into a prophecy of Messianic judgment and bliss, and she ends with a comforting message:

> But when all things become an ashy pile,
> God will put out the fire unspeakable
> Which he once kindled, and the bones and ashes
> Of men will God himself again transform,
> And raise up mortals as they were before.
> And then will be the judgment, God himself
> Will sit as judge, and judge the world again.
> As many as committed impious sins
> Shall Stygian Gehenna's depths conceal
> 'Neath molten earth and dismal Tartarus.
>
> But the pious shall again live on the earth,
> And God will give them spirit, life, and means
> Of nourishment, and all shall see themselves,
> Beholding the sun's sweet and cheerful light.
> O happiest men who at that time shall live!

The Jews found some consolation for present sorrows in the thought of past deliverances. The short historical record known as the "Scroll of Fasting" (*Megillath Taanith*) was perhaps begun before the destruction of the Temple, but was completed after the death of Trajan in 118. This scroll contained thirty-five brief paragraphs written in Aramaic. The compilation, which is of great historical value, follows the order of the Jewish Calendar, beginning with the month Nisan and ending with Adar. The entries in the list relate to the days on which it was held unlawful to fast, and many of these days were anniversaries of national victories. The Megillath Taanith contains no jubilations over these triumphs, but is a sober record of facts. It is a precious survival of the historical works compiled by the Jews before their dispersion from Palestine. Such works differ from those of Josephus and the Sibyl in their motive. They were not designed to win foreign admiration for Judaism, but to provide an accurate record for home use and inspire the Jews with hope amid the threatening prospects of life.

* * * * *

BIBLIOGRAPHY

JOSEPHUS.

Whiston's English Translation, revised by Shilleto (1889).
Graetz.—II, p. 276 [278].

SIBYLLINE ORACLES.

S.A. Hirsch.—*Jewish Sibylline Oracles, J.Q.R.*, II, p. 406.

CHAPTER III

THE TALMUD

I (220-280) Palestine—Jochanan, Simon, Joshua, Simlai; Babylonia—Rab and Samuel.

II (280-320) Palestine—Ami, Assi, Abbahu, Chiya; Babylonia—Huna and Zeira.

III (320-380) Babylonia—Rabba, Abayi, Rava.

IV (380-430) Babylonia—Ashi (first compilation of the Babylonian Talmud).

V and VI (430-500) Babylonia—Rabina (completion of the Babylonian Talmud).

The *Talmud*, or *Gemara* ("Doctrine," or "Completion"), was a natural development of the Mishnah. The Talmud contains, indeed, many elements as old as the Mishnah, some even older. But, considered as a whole, the Talmud is a commentary on the work of the Tannaim. It is written, not in Hebrew, as the Mishnah is, but in a popular Aramaic. There are two distinct works to which the title Talmud is applied; the one is the Jerusalem Talmud (completed about the year 370 C.E.), the other the Babylonian (completed a century later). At first, as we have seen, the Rabbinical schools were founded on Jewish soil. But Palestine did not continue to offer a friendly welcome. Under the more tolerant rulers of Babylonia or Persia, Jewish learning found a refuge from the harshness experienced under those of the Holy Land. The Babylonian Jewish schools in Nehardea, Sura, and Pumbeditha rapidly surpassed the Palestinian in reputation, and in the year 350 C.E., owing to natural decay, the Palestinian schools closed.

The Talmud is accordingly not one work, but two, the one the literary product of the Palestinian, the other, of the Babylonian *Amoraim*. The latter is the larger, the more studied, the better preserved, and to it attention will here be mainly confined. The Talmud is not a book, it is a literature. It contains a legal code, a system of ethics, a body of ritual customs, poetical passages, prayers, histories, facts of science and medicine, and fancies of folk-lore.

The Amoraim were what their name implies, "Expounders," or "Discoursers"; but their expositions were often original contributions to literature. Their work extends over the long interval between 200 and 500 C.E. The Amoraim naturally were men of various character and condition. Some were possessed of much material wealth, others were excessively poor. But few of them were professional men of letters. Like the Tannaim, the Amoraim were often artisans, field-laborers, or physicians, whose heart was certainly in literature, but whose hand was turned to the practical affairs of life. The men who stood highest socially, the Princes of the Captivity in Babylonia and the Patriarchs in Palestine, were not always those vested with the highest authority. Some of the Amoraim, again, were merely receptive, the medium through which tradition was handed on; others were creative as well. To put the same fact in Rabbinical metaphor, some were Sinais of learning, others tore up mountains, and ground them together in keen and critical dialectics.

The oldest of the Amoraim, Chanina, the son of Chama, of Sepphoris (180-260), was such a firm mountain of ancient learning. On the other hand, Jochanan, the son of Napacha (199-279), of dazzling physical beauty, had a more original mind. His personal charms conveyed to him perhaps a sense of the artistic; to him the Greek language was a delight, "an ornament of women." Simon, the son of Lakish (200-275), hardy of muscle and of intellect, started life as a professional athlete. A later Rabbi, Zeira, was equally noted for his feeble, unprepossessing figure and his nimble, ingenious mind. Another contemporary of Jochanan, Joshua, the son of Levi, is the hero of many legends. He was so tender to the poor that he declared his conviction that the Messiah would arise among the beggars and cripples of Rome. Simlai, who was born in Palestine, and migrated to Nehardea in Babylonia, was more of a poet than a lawyer. His love was for the ethical and poetic elements of the Talmud, the *Hagadah*, as this aspect of the Rabbinical literature was called in contradistinction to the *Halachah*, or legal elements. Simlai entered into frequent discussions with the Christian Fathers on subjects of Biblical exegesis.

The centre of interest now changes to Babylonia. Here, in the year 219, Abba Areka, or Rab (175-247), founded the Sura academy, which continued to flourish for nearly eight centuries. He and his great contemporary Samuel (180-257) enjoy with Jochanan the honor of supplying the leading materials of which the Talmud consists. Samuel laid down a rule which, based on an utterance of the prophet Jeremiah, enabled Jews to live and serve in non-Jewish countries. "The law of the land is law," said Samuel. But he lived in the realms of the stars as well as in the streets of his city. Samuel was an astronomer, and he is reported to have boasted with truth, that "he was as familiar with the paths of the stars as with the streets of Nehardea." He arranged the Jewish Calendar, his work in this direction being perfected by Hillel II in the fourth century. Like Simlai, Rab and Samuel had heathen and Christian friends. Origen and Jerome read the Scriptures under the guidance of Jews. The heathen philosopher Porphyry wrote a commentary on the Book of Daniel. So, too, Abbahu, who lived in Palestine a little later on, frequented the society of cultivated Romans, and had his family taught Greek. Abbahu was a manufacturer of veils for women's wear, for, like many Amoraim, he scorned to make learning a means of living, Abbahu's modesty with regard to his own merits shows that a Rabbi was not necessarily arrogant in pride of knowledge! Once Abbahu's lecture was besieged by a great crowd, but the audience of his colleague Chiya was scanty. "Thy teaching," said Abbahu to Chiya, "is a rare jewel, of which only an expert can judge; mine is tinsel, which attracts every ignorant eye."

It was Rab, however, who was the real popularizer of Jewish learning. He arranged courses of lectures for the people as well as for scholars. Rab's successor as head of the Sura school, Huna (212-297), completed Rab's work in making Babylonia the chief centre of Jewish learning. Huna tilled his own fields for a living, and might often be met going home with his spade over his shoulder. It was men like this who built up the Jewish tradition. Huna's predecessor, however, had wider experience of life, for Rab had been a student in Palestine, and was in touch with the Jews of many parts. From Rab's time onwards, learning became the property of the whole people, and the Talmud, besides being the literature of the Jewish universities, may be called the book of the masses. It contains, not only the legal and ethical results of the investigations of the learned, but also the wisdom and superstition of the masses. The Talmud is not exactly a national literature, but it was a unique bond between the scattered Jews, an unparallelled spiritual and literary instrument for maintaining the identity of Judaism amid the many tribulations to which the Jews were subjected.

The Talmud owed much to many minds. Externally it was influenced by the nations with which the Jews came into contact. From the inside, the influences at work were equally various. Jochanan, Rab, and Samuel in the third century prepared the material out of which the Talmud was finally built. The actual building was done by scholars in the fourth century. Rabba, the son of Nachmani (270-330), Abayi (280-338), and Rava (299-352) gave the finishing touches to the method of the Talmud. Rabba was a man of the people; he was a clear thinker, and loved to attract all comers by an apt anecdote. Rava had a superior sense of his own dignity, and rather neglected the needs of the ordinary man of his day. Abayi was more of the type of the average Rabbi, acute, genial, self-denying. Under the impulse of men of the most various gifts of mind and heart, the Talmud was gradually constructed, but two names are prominently associated with its actual compilation. These were Ashi (352-427) and Rabina (died 499). Ashi combined massive learning with keen logical ingenuity. He needed both for the task to which he devoted half a century of his life. He possessed a vast memory, in which the accumulated tradition of six centuries was stored, and he was gifted with the mental orderliness which empowered him to deal with this bewildering mass of materials.

It is hardly possible that after the compilation of the Talmud it remained an oral book, though it must be remembered that memory played a much greater part in earlier centuries than it does now. At all events, Ashi, and after him Rabina, performed the great work of systematizing the Rabbinical literature at a turning-point in the world's history. The Mishnah had been begun at a moment when the Roman empire was at its greatest vigor and glory; the Talmud was completed at the time when the Roman empire was in its decay. That the Jews were saved from similar disintegration, was due very largely to the Talmud. The Talmud is thus one of the great books of the world. Despite its faults, its excessive casuistry, its lack of style and form, its stupendous mass of detailed laws and restrictions, it is nevertheless a great book in and for itself. It is impossible to consider it further here in its religious aspects. But something must be said in the next chapter of that side of the Rabbinical literature known as the *Midrash*.

* * * * *

BIBLIOGRAPHY

THE TALMUD.

Essays by E. Deutsch and A. Darmesteter (Jewish Publication Society of America).

Graetz.—II, 18-22 (character of the Talmud, end of ch. 22).

Karpeles.—*Jewish Literature and other Essays*, p. 52.

Steinschneider.—*Jewish Literature*, p. 20.

Schiller-Szinessy.—*Encycl. Brit.*, Vol. XXIII, p. 35.

M. Mielziner.—*Introduction to the Talmud* (Cincinnati, 1894).

S. Schechter.—*Some Aspects of Rabbinic Theology, J.Q.R.*, VI, p. 405, etc.

—*Studies in Judaism* (Jewish Publication Society of America, 1896), pp. 155, 182, 213, 233 [189, 222, 259, 283].

B. Spiers.—*School System of the Talmud* (London, 1898) (with appendix on Baba Kama); the *Threefold Cord* (1893) on *Sanhedrin, Baba Metsia*, and *Baba Bathra*.

M. Jastrow.—*History and Future of the Text of the Talmud* (*Publications of the Gratz College*, Philadelphia, 1897, Vol. I).

P.B. Benny.—*Criminal Code of the Jews according to the Talmud* (London, 1880).

S. Mendelsohn.—*The Criminal Jurisprudence of the Ancient Hebrews* (Baltimore, 1891).

D. Castelli.—*Future Life in Rabbinical Literature, J.Q.R.*, I, p. 314.

M. Güdemann.—*Spirit and Letter in Judaism and Christianity*, *ibid.*, IV, p. 345.

I. Harris.—*Rise and Development of the Massorah*, *ibid.*, I, pp. 128, etc.

H. Polano.—*The Talmud* (Philadelphia, 1876).

I. Myers.—*Gems from the Talmud* (London, 1894).

D.W. Amram.—*The Jewish Law of Divorce according to Bible and Talmud* (Philadelphia, 1896).

CHAPTER IV

THE MIDRASH AND ITS POETRY

Mechilta, Sifra, Sifre, Pesikta, Tanchuma, Midrash Rabbah, Yalkut.—Proverbs.—Parables.—Fables.

In its earliest forms identical with the Halachah, or the practical and legal aspects of the Mishnah and the Talmud, the Midrash, in its fuller development, became an independent branch of Rabbinical literature. Like the Talmud, the Midrash is of a composite nature, and under the one name the accumulations of ages are included. Some of its contents are earlier than the completion of the Bible, others were collected and even created as recently as the tenth or the eleventh century of the current era.

Midrash ("Study," "Inquiry") was in the first instance an *Explanation of the Scriptures*. This explanation is often the clear, natural exposition of the text, and it enforces rules of conduct both ethical and ritual. The historical and moral traditions which clustered round the incidents and characters of the Bible soon received a more vivid setting. The poetical sense of the Rabbis expressed itself in a vast and beautiful array of legendary additions to the Bible, but the additions are always devised with a moral purpose, to give point to a preacher's homily or to inspire the imagination of the audience with nobler fancies. Besides being expository, the Midrash is, therefore, didactic and poetical, the moral being conveyed in the guise of a *narrative*, amplifying and developing the contents of Scripture. The Midrash gives the results of that deep searching of the Scriptures which became second nature with the

Jews, and it also represents the changes and expansions of ethical and theological ideals as applied to a changing and growing life.

From another point of view, also, the Midrash is a poetical literature. Its function as a species of *popular homiletics* made it necessary to appeal to the emotions. In its warm and living application of abstract truths to daily ends, in its responsive and hopeful intensification of the nearness of God to Israel, in its idealization of the past and future of the Jews, it employed the poet's art in essence, though not in form. It will be seen later on that in another sense the Midrash is a poetical literature, using the lore of the folk, the parable, the proverb, the allegory, and the fable, and often using them in the language of poetry.

The oldest Midrash is the actual report of sermons and addresses of the Tannaite age; the latest is a medieval compilation from all extant sources. The works to which the name Midrash is applied are the *Mechilta* (to Exodus); the *Sifra* (to Leviticus); the *Sifre* (to Numbers and Deuteronomy); the *Pesikta* (to various *Sections* of the Bible, whence its name); the *Tanchuma* (to the Pentateuch); the *Midrash Rabbah* (the "Great Midrash," to the Pentateuch and the Five Scrolls of Esther, Ruth, Lamentations, Ecclesiastes, and the Song of Songs); and the *Midrash Haggadol* (identical in name, and in contents similar to, but not identical with, the *Midrash Rabbah*); together with a large number of collected Midrashim, such as the *Yalkut*, and a host of smaller works, several of which are no longer extant.

Regarding the Midrash in its purely literary aspects, we find its style to be far more lucid than that of the Talmud, though portions of the Halachic Midrash are identical in character with the Talmud. The Midrash has many passages in which the simple graces of form match the beauty of idea. But for the most part the style is simple and prosaic, rather than ornate or poetical. It produces its effects by the most straightforward means, and strikes a modern reader as lacking distinction in form. The dead level of commonplace expression is, however, brightened by brilliant passages of frequent occurrence. Prayers, proverbs, parables, and fables, dot the pages of Talmud and Midrash alike. The ancient *proverbs* of the Jews were more than mere chips from the block of experience. They were poems, by reason of their use of metaphor, alliteration, assonance, and imagination. The Rabbinical proverbs show all these poetical qualities.

> He who steals from a thief smells of theft.—Charity is the salt of Wealth.—Silence is a fence about Wisdom.—Many old camels carry the skins of their young.—Two dry sticks and one green burn together.—If the priest steals the god, on what can one take an oath?—All the dyers cannot bleach a raven's wing.—Into a well from which you have drunk, cast no stone.—Alas for the bread which the baker calls bad.—Slander is a Snake that stings in Syria, and slays in Rome.—The Dove escaped from the Eagle and found a Serpent in her nest.—Tell no secrets, for the Wall has ears.

These, like many more of the Rabbinical proverbs, are essentially poetical. Some, indeed, are either expanded metaphors or metaphors touched by genius into poetry. The alliterative proverbs and maxims of the Talmud and Midrash are less easily illustrated. Sometimes they enshrine a pun or a conceit, or depend for their aptness upon an assonance. In some of the Talmudic proverbs there is a spice of cynicism. But most of them show a genial attitude towards life.

The poetical proverb easily passes into the parable. Loved in Bible times, the parable became in after centuries the most popular form of didactic poetry among the Jews. The Bible has its parables, but the Midrash overflows with them. They are occasionally re-workings of older thoughts, but mostly they are original creations, invented for a special purpose, stories devised to drive home a moral, allegories administering in pleasant wrappings unpalatable satires or admonitions. In all ages up to the present, Jewish moralists have relied on the parable as their most effective instrument. The poetry of the Jewish parables is characteristic also of the parables imitated from the Jewish, but the latter have a distinguishing feature peculiar to them. This is their humor, the witty or humorous parable being exclusively Jewish. The parable is less spontaneous than the proverb. It is a product of moral poetry rather than of folk wisdom. Yet the parable was so like the proverb that the moral of a parable often became a new proverb. The diction of the parable is naturally more ornate. By the beauty of its expression, its frequent application of rural incidents to the life familiar in the cities, the rhythm and flow of its periods, its fertile imagination, the parable should certainly be placed high in the world's poetry. But it was poetry with a *tendency*, the *mashal*, or proverb-parable, being what the Rabbis themselves termed it, "the clear small light by which lost jewels can be found."

The following is a parable of Hillel, which is here cited more to mention that noble, gentle Sage than as a specimen of this class of literature. Hillel belongs to a period earlier than that dealt with in this book, but his loving and pure spirit breathes through the pages of the Talmud and Midrash:

> Hillel, the gentle, the beloved sage,
> Expounded day by day the sacred page
> To his disciples in the house of learning;
> And day by day, when home at eve returning,
> They lingered, clustering round him, loth to part
> From him whose gentle rule won every heart.
> But evermore, when they were wont to plead
> For longer converse, forth he went with speed,
> Saying each day: "I go—the hour is late—
> To tend the guest who doth my coming wait,"
> Until at last they said: "The Rabbi jests,
> When telling us thus daily of his guests
> That wait for him." The Rabbi paused awhile,
> And then made answer: "Think you I beguile
> You with an idle tale? Not so, forsooth!
> I have a guest whom I must tend in truth.
> Is not the soul of man indeed a guest,
> Who in this body deigns a while to rest,
> And dwells with me all peacefully to-day:
> To-morrow—may it not have fled away?"

Space must be found for one other parable, taken (like many other poetical quotations in this volume) from Mrs. Lucas' translations:

> Simeon ben Migdal, at the close of day,
> Upon the shores of ocean chanced to stray,

And there a man of form and mien uncouth,
Dwarfed and misshapen, met he on the way.

"Hail, Rabbi," spoke the stranger passing by,
But Simeon thus, discourteous, made reply:
"Say, are there in thy city many more,
Like unto thee, an insult to the eye?"

"Nay, that I cannot tell," the wand'rer said,
"But if thou wouldst ply the scorner's trade,
Go first and ask the Master Potter why
He has a vessel so misshapen made?"

Then (so the legend tells) the Rabbi knew
That he had sinned, and prone himself he threw
Before the other's feet, and prayed of him
Pardon for the words that now his soul did rue.

But still the other answered as before:
"Go, in the Potter's ear thy plaint outpour,
For what am I! His hand has fashioned me,
And I in humble faith that hand adore."

Brethren, do we not often too forget
Whose hand it is that many a time has set
A radiant soul in an unlovely form,
A fair white bird caged in a mouldering net?

Nay more, do not life's times and chances, sent
By the great Artificer with intent
That they should prove a blessing, oft appear
To us a burden that we sore lament?

Ah! soul, poor soul of man! what heavenly fire
Would thrill thy depths and love of God inspire,
Could'st thou but see the Master hand revealed,
Majestic move "earth's scheme of things entire."

It cannot be! Unseen he guideth us,
But yet our feeble hands, the luminous

Pure lamp of faith can light to glorify
The narrow path that he has traced for us.

Finally, there are the *Beast Fables* of the Talmud and the Midrash. Most of these were borrowed directly or indirectly from India. We are told in the Talmud that Rabbi Meir knew three hundred Fox Fables, and that with his death (about 290 C.E.) "fabulists ceased to be," Very few of Meir's fables are extant, so that it is impossible to gather whether or not they were original. There are only thirty fables in the Talmud and the Midrash, and of these several cannot be parallelled in other literatures. Some of the Talmudic fables are found also in the classical and the earliest Indian collections; some in the later collections; some in the classics, but not in the Indian lists; some in India, but not in the Latin and Greek authors. Among the latter is the well-known fable of the *Fox and the Fishes*, used so dramatically by Rabbi Akiba. The original Talmudic fables are, according to Mr. J. Jacobs, the following: *Chaff, Straw, and Wheat*, who dispute for which of them the seed has been sown: the winnowing fan soon decides; *The Caged Bird*, who is envied by his free fellow; *The Wolf and the two Hounds*, who have quarrelled; the wolf seizes one, the other goes to his rival's aid, fearing the same fate himself on the morrow, unless he helps the other dog to-day; *The Wolf at the Well*, the mouth of the well is covered with a net: "If I go down into the well," says the wolf, "I shall be caught. If I do not descend, I shall die of thirst"; *The Cock and the Bat*, who sit together waiting for the sunrise: "I wait for the dawn," said the cock, "for the light is my signal; but as for thee—the light is thy ruin"; and, finally, what Mr. Jacobs calls the grim beast-tale of the *Fox as Singer*, in which the beasts—invited by the lion to a feast, and covered by him with the skins of wild beasts—are led by the fox in a chorus: "What has happened to those above us, will happen to him above," implying that their host, too, will come to a violent death. In the context the fable is applied to Haman, whose fate, it is augured, will resemble that of the two officers whose guilt Mordecai detected.

Such fables are used in the Talmud to point religious or even political morals, very much as the parables were. The fable, however, took a lower flight than the parable, and its moral was based on expediency, rather than on the highest ethical ideals. The importance of the Talmudic fables is historical more than literary or religious. Hebrew fables supply one of the links connecting the popular literature of the East with that of the West. But they hardly belong in the true sense to Jewish literature. Parables, on the other hand, were an essential and characteristic branch of that literature.

* * * * *

BIBLIOGRAPHY

MIDRASH.

> Schiller-Szinessy.—*Encycl. Brit.*, Vol. XVI, p. 285.
> Graetz.—II, p. 328 [331] *seq.*
> Steinschneider.—*Jewish Literature*, pp. 5 *seq.*, 36 *seq.*
> L.N. Dembitz.—*Jewish Services in Synagogue and Home* (Jewish Publication Society of America, 1898), p. 44.

FABLES.

> J. Jacobs.—*The Fables of Æsop* (London, 1889), I, p. 110 *seq.*
> Read also Schechter, *Studies in Judaism*, p. 272 [331]; and *J.Q.R.*, (Kohler), V, p. 399; VII, p. 581; (Bacher) IV, p. 406; (Davis) VIII, p. 529; (Abrahams) I, p. 216; II, p. 172; Chenery, *Legends from the Midrash* (*Miscellany of the Society of Hebrew Literature*, Vol. II).

CHAPTER V

THE LETTERS OF THE GAONIM

Representative Gaonim:
Achai, Amram, Zemach, Saadiah, Sherira, Samuel, Hai.

For several centuries after the completion of the Talmud, Babylonia or Persia continued to hold the supremacy in Jewish learning. The great teachers in the Persian schools followed the same lines as their predecessors in the Mishnah and the Talmud. Their name was changed more than their character. The title *Gaon* ("Excellence") was applied to the head of the school, the members of which devoted themselves mainly to the study and interpretation of the older literature. They also made original contributions to the store. Of their extensive works but little has been preserved. What has survived proves that they were gifted with the faculty of applying old precept to modern instance. They regulated the social and religious affairs of all the Jews in the diaspora. They improved educational methods, and were pioneers in the popularization of learning. By a large collection of Case Law, that is, decisions in particular cases, they brought the newer Jewish life into moral harmony with the principles formulated by the earlier Rabbis. The Gaonim were the originators or, at least, the arrangers of parts of the liturgy. They composed new hymns and invocations, fixed the order of service, and established in full vigor a system of *Minhag*, or Custom, whose power became more and more predominant, not only in religious, but also in social and commercial affairs.

The literary productions of the Gaonic age open with the *Sheeltoth* written by Achai in the year 760. This, the first independent book composed after the close of the Talmud, was curiously enough compiled in Palestine, whither Achai had migrated from Persia. The Sheeltoth ("Inquiries") contain nearly two hundred homilies on the Pentateuch. In the year 880 another Gaon, Amram by name, prepared a *Siddur*, or Prayer-Book, which includes many remarks on the history of the liturgy and the customs connected with it. A contemporary of Amram, Zemach, the son of Paltoi, found a different channel for his literary energies. He compiled an *Aruch*, or Talmudical Lexicon. Of the most active of the Gaonim, Saadiah, more will be said in a subsequent chapter. We will now pass on to Sherira, who in 987 wrote his famous "Letter," containing a history of the Jewish Tradition, a work which stamps the author as at once learned and critical. It shows that the Gaonim were not afraid nor incapable of facing such problems as this: Was the Mishnah *orally* transmitted to the Amoraim (or Rabbis of the Talmud), or was it *written down* by the compiler? Sherira accepted the former alternative. The latest Gaonim were far more productive than the earlier. Samuel, the son of Chofni, who died in 1034, and the last of the Gaonim, Hai, who flourished from 998 to 1038, were the authors of many works on the Talmud, the Bible, and other branches of Jewish literature. Hai Gaon was also a poet.

The language used by the Gaonim was at first Hebrew and Aramaic, and the latter remained the official speech of the Gaonate. In course of time, Arabic replaced the Aramean dialect, and became the *lingua franca* of the Jews.

The formal works of the Gaonim, with certain obvious exceptions, were not, however, the writings by which they left their mark on their age. The most original and important of the Gaonic writings were their "Letters," or "Answers" (*Teshuboth*). The Gaonim, as heads of the school in the Babylonian cities Sura and Pumbeditha, enjoyed far more than local authority. The Jews of Persia were practically independent of external control. Their official heads were the Exilarchs, who reigned over the Jews as viceroys of the caliphs. The Gaonim were the religious heads of an emancipated community. The Exilarchs possessed a princely revenue, which they devoted in part to the schools over which the Gaonim presided. This position of authority, added to the world-wide repute of the two schools, gave the Gaonim an influence which extended beyond their own neighborhood. From all parts of the Jewish world their guidance was sought and their opinions solicited on a vast variety of subjects, mainly, but not exclusively, religious and literary. Amid the growing complications of ritual law, a desire was felt for terse prescriptions, clear-cut decisions, and rules of conduct. The imperfections of study outside of Persia, again, made it essential to apply to the Gaonim for authoritative expositions of difficult passages in the Bible and the Talmud. To all such enquiries the Gaonim sent responses in the form of letters, sometimes addressed to individual correspondents, sometimes to communities or groups of communities. These Letters and other compilations containing Halachic (or practical) decisions were afterwards collected into treatises, such as the "Great Rules" (*Halachoth Gedoloth*), originally compiled in the eighth century, but subsequently reedited. Mostly, however, the Letters were left in loose form, and were collected in much later times.

The Letters of the Gaonim have little pretence to literary form. They are the earliest specimens of what became a very characteristic branch of Jewish literature. "Questions and Answers" (*Shaaloth u-Teshuboth*) abound in later times in all Jewish circles, and there is no real parallel to them in any other literature. More will be said later on as to these curious works. So far as the Gaonic period is concerned, the characteristics of these thousands of letters are lucidity of thought and terseness of expression. The Gaonim never waste a word. They are rarely over-bearing in manner, but mostly use a tone which is persuasive rather than disciplinary. The Gaonim were, in this real sense, therefore, princes of letter-writing. Moreover, though their Letters deal almost entirely with contemporary affairs, they now constitute as fresh and vivid reading as when first penned. Subjected to the severe test of time, the Letters of the Gaonim emerge triumphant.

* * * * *

BIBLIOGRAPHY

GAONIM.

> Graetz.—III, 4-8.
> Steinschneider.—*Jewish Literature*, p. 25.

CHAPTER VI

THE KARAITIC LITERATURE

Anan, Nahavendi, Abul-Faraj, Salman, Sahal, al-Bazir, Hassan, Japhet, Kirkisani, Judah Hadassi, Isaac Troki.

In the very heart of the Gaonate, the eighth century witnessed a religious and literary reaction against Rabbinism. The opposition to the Rabbinite spirit was far older than this, but it came to a head under Anan, the son of David, the founder of Karaism. Anan had been an unsuccessful candidate for the dignity of Exilarch, and thus personal motives were involved in his attack on the Gaonim. But there were other reasons for the revolt. In the same century, Islam, like Judaism, was threatened by a fierce antagonism between the friends and the foes of tradition. In Islam the struggle lay between the Sunnites, who interpreted Mohammedanism in accordance with authorized tradition, and the Shiites, who relied exclusively upon the Koran. Similarly, in Judaism, the Rabbinites obeyed the traditions of the earlier authorities, and the Karaites (from *Kera*, or *Mikra*, i.e. "Bible") claimed the right to reject tradition and revert to the Bible as the original source of inspiration. Such reactions against tradition are recurrent in all religions.

Karaism, however, was not a true reaction against tradition. It replaced an old tradition by a new one; it substituted a rigid, unprogressive authority for one capable of growth and adaptation to changing requirements. In the end, Karaism became so hedged in by its supposed avoidance of tradition that it ceased to be a living force. But we are here not concerned with the religious defects of Karaism. Regarded from the literary side, Karaism produced a double effect. Karaism itself gave birth to an original and splendid literature, and, on the other hand, coming as it did at the time when Arabic science and poetry were attaining their golden zenith, Karaism aroused within the Rabbinite sphere a notable energy, which resulted in some of the best work of medieval Jews.

Among the most famous of the Karaite authors was Benjamin Nahavendi, who lived at the beginning of the ninth century, and displayed much resolution and ability as an advocate of free-thought in religion. Nahavendi not only wrote commentaries on the Bible, but also attempted to write a philosophy of Judaism, being allied to Philo in the past and to the Arabic writers in his own time. At the end of the ninth century, Abul-Faraj Harun made a great stride forwards as an expounder of the Bible and as an authority on Hebrew grammar.

During the ninth and tenth centuries, several Karaites revealed much vigor and ability in their controversies with the Gaonim. In this field the most distinguished Karaitic writers were Salman, the son of Yerucham (885-960); Sahal, the son of Mazliach (900-950); Joseph al-Bazir (flourished 910-930); Hassan, the son of Mashiach (930); and Japhet, the son of Ali (950-990).

Salman, the son of Yerucham, was an active traveller; born in Egypt, he went as a young man to Jerusalem, which he made his head-quarters for several years, though he paid occasional visits to Babylonia and to his native land. These journeys helped to unify the scattered Karaite communities. Besides his Biblical works, Salman composed a poetical treatise against the Rabbinite theories. To this book, which was written in Hebrew, Salman gave the title, "The Wars of the Lord." — was he a Moslem?

Sahal, the son of Mazliach, on the other hand, was a native of the Holy Land, and though an eager polemical writer against the Rabbinites, he bore a smaller part than Salman in the practical development of Karaism. His "Hebrew Grammar" (*Sefer Dikduk*) and his Lexicon (*Leshon Limmudim*) were very popular. Unlike the work of other Karaites, Joseph al-Bazir's writings were philosophical, and had no philological value. He was an adherent of the Mohammedan theological method known as the Kalam, and wrote mostly in Arabic. Another Karaite of the same period, Hassan, the son of Mashiach, was the one who impelled Saadiah to throw off all reserves and enter the lists as a champion of Rabbinism.

Of the remaining Karaites of the tenth century, the foremost was Japhet, the son of Ali, whose commentaries on the Bible represent the highest achievements of Karaism. A large Hebrew dictionary (*Iggaron*), by a contemporary of Japhet named David, the son of Abraham, is also a work which was often quoted. Kirkisani, also a tenth century Karaite, completed in the year 937 a treatise called, "The Book of Lights and the High Beacons." In this work much valuable information is supplied as to the history of Karaism. Despite his natural prejudices in favor of his own sect, Kirkisani is a faithful historian, as frank regarding the internal dissensions of the Karaites as in depicting the divergence of views among the Rabbinites. Kirkisani's work is thus of the greatest importance for the history of Jewish sects.

Finally, the famous Karaite Judah Hadassi (1075-1160) was a young man when his native Jerusalem was stormed by the Crusaders in 1099. A wanderer to Constantinople, he devoted himself to science, Hebrew philology, and Greek literature. He utilized his wide knowledge in his great work, "A Cluster of Cyprus Flowers" (*Eshkol ha-Kopher*), which was completed in 1150. It is written in a series of rhymed alphabetical acrostics. It is encyclopedic in range, and treats critically, not only of Judaism, but also of Christianity and Islam.

Karaitic literature was produced in later centuries also, but by the end of the twelfth century, Karaism had exhausted its originality and fertility. One much later product of Karaism, however, deserves special mention. Isaac Troki composed, in 1593, a work entitled "The Strengthening of Faith" (*Chizzuk Emunah*), in which the author defended Judaism and attacked Christianity. It was a lucid book, and as its arguments were popularly arranged, it was very much read and used. With this exception, Karaism produced no important work after the twelfth century.

On the intellectual side, therefore, Karaism was a powerful though ephemeral movement. In several branches of science and philology the Karaites made real additions to contemporary knowledge. But the main service of Karaism was indirect. The Rabbinite Jews, who represented the mass of the people, had been on the way to a scientific and philosophical development of their own before the rise of Karaism. The necessity of fighting Karaism with its own weapons gave a strong impetus to the new movement in Rabbinism, and some of the best work of Saadiah was inspired by Karaitic opposition. Before, however, we turn to the career of Saadiah, we must consider another literary movement, which coincided in date with the rise of Karaism, but was entirely independent of it.

* * * * *

BIBLIOGRAPHY

KARAITES.

> Graetz.—III, 5 (on Troki, *ibid.*, IV, 18, end. M. Mocatta, *Faith Strengthened*, London, 1851).
> Steinschneider.—*Jewish Literature*, p. 115 *seq.*
> W. Bacher.—*Qirqisani the Qaraite, and his Work on Jewish Sects*, *J.Q.R.*, VII, p. 687.
> —*Jehuda Hadassi's Eshkol Hakkofer*, *J.Q.R.*, VIII, p. 431.
> S. Poznanski.—*Karaite Miscellanies*, *J.Q.R.*, VIII, p. 681.

CHAPTER VII

THE NEW-HEBREW PIYUT

Kalirian and Spanish Piyutim (Poems).—Jannai.—Kalir.

Arabic to a large extent replaced Hebrew as the literary language of the Jews, but Hebrew continued the language of prayer. As a mere literary form, Rabbinic Hebrew retained a strong hold on the Jews; as a vehicle of devotional feeling, Hebrew reigned supreme. The earliest additions to the fixed liturgy of the Synagogue were prose-poems. They were "Occasional Prayers" composed by the precentor for a special occasion. An appropriate melody or chant accompanied the new hymn, and if the poem and melody met the popular taste, both won a permanent place in the local liturgy. The hymns were unrhymed and unmetrical, but they may have been written in the form of alphabetical acrostics, such as appear in the 119th and a few other Psalms.

It is not impossible that metre and rhyme grew naturally from the Biblical Hebrew. Rhyme is unknown in the Bible, but the assonances which occur may easily run into rhymes. Musical form is certainly present in Hebrew poetry, though strict metres are foreign to it. As an historical fact, however, Hebrew rhymed verse can be traced on the one side to Syriac, on the other to Arabic influences. In the latter case the influence was external only. Early Arabic poetry treats of war and love, but the first Jewish rhymsters sang of peace and duty. The Arab wrote for the camp, the Jew for the synagogue.

Two distinct types of verse, or *Piyut* (i.e. Poetry), arose within the Jewish circle: the ingenious and the natural. In the former, the style is rugged and involved; a profusion of rare words and obscure allusions meets and troubles the reader; the verse lacks all beauty of form, yet is alive with intense spiritual force. This style is often termed Kalirian, from the name of its best representative. The Kalirian Piyut in the end spread chiefly to France, England, Burgundy, Lorraine, Germany, Bohemia, Poland, Italy, Greece, and Palestine. The other type of new-Hebrew Piyut, the Spanish, rises to higher beauties of form. It is not free from the Kalirian faults, but it has them in a less pronounced degree. The Spanish Piyut, in the hands of one or two masters, becomes true poetry, poetry in form as well as in idea. The Spanish style prevailed in Castile, Andalusia, Catalonia, Aragon, Majorca, Provence, and in countries where Arabic influence was strongest.

Kalir was the most popular writer of the earlier type of new-Hebrew poetry, but he was not its creator. An older contemporary of his, from whom he derived both his diction and his method of treating poetic subjects, was Jannai. Though we know that Jannai was a prolific writer, only seven short examples of his verse remain. One of these is the popular hymn, "It was at Midnight," which is still recited by "German" Jews at the home-service on the first eve of Passover. It recounts in order the deliverances which, according to the Midrash, were wrought for Israel at midnight, from Abraham's victory over the four kings to the wakefulness of Ahasuerus, the crisis of the Book of Esther. In the last stanza is a prayer for future redemption:

> Bring nigh the hour which is nor day nor night!
> Most High! make known that thine is day, and thine the
> night!
> Make clear as day the darkness of our night!
> As of old at midnight.

This form of versification, with a running refrain, afterwards became very popular with Jewish poets. Jannai also displays the harsh alliterations, the learned allusions to Midrash and Talmud, which were carried to extremes by Kalir.

It is strange that it is impossible to fix with any certainty the date at which Jannai and Kalir lived. Kalir may belong to the eighth or to the ninth century. It is equally hard to decide as to his birth-place. Rival theories hold that he was born in Palestine and in Sardinia. His name has been derived from Cagliari in Sardinia and from the Latin *calyrum*, a cake. Honey-cakes were given to Jewish children on their first introduction to school, and the nickname "Kaliri," or "Boy of the Cake," may have arisen from his youthful precocity. But all this is mere guess-work.

It is more certain that the poet was also the singer of his own verses. His earliest audiences were probably scholars, and this may have tempted Kalir to indulge in the recondite learning which vitiates his hymns. At his worst, Kalir is very bad indeed; his style is then a jumble of words, his meaning obscure and even unintelligible. He uses a maze of alphabetical acrostics, line by line he wreathes into his compositions the words of successive Bible texts. Yet even at his worst he is ingenious and vigorous. Such phrases as "to hawk it as a hawk upon a sparrow" are at least bold and effective. Ibn Ezra later on lamented that Kalir had treated the Hebrew language like an unfenced city. But if the poet too freely admitted strange and ugly words, he added many of considerable force and beauty. Kalir rightly felt that if Hebrew was to remain a living tongue, it was absurd to restrict the language to the vocabulary of the Bible. Hence he invented many new verbs from nouns.

But his inventiveness was less marked than his learning. "With the permission of God, I will speak in riddles," says Kalir in opening the prayer for dew. The riddles are mainly clever allusions to the Midrash. It has been pointed out that these allusions are often tasteless and obscure. But they are more often beautiful and inspiring. No Hebrew poet in the Middle Ages was illiterate, for the poetic instinct was fed on the fancies of the Midrash. This accounts for their lack of freshness and originality. The poet was a scholar, and he was also a teacher. Much of Kalir's work is didactic; it teaches the traditional explanations of the Bible and the ritual laws for Sabbath and festivals; it provides a convenient summary of the six hundred and thirteen precepts into which the duties of the Law were arranged. But over and above all this the genius of Kalir soars to poetic heights. So much has been said of Kalir's obscurity that one quotation must, in fairness be given of Kalir at his simplest and best. The passage is taken from a hymn sung on the seventh day of Tabernacles, the day of the great Hosannas:

O give ear to the prayer of those who long for thy
     salvation,
Rejoicing before thee with the willows of the brook,
     And save us now!

O redeem the vineyard which thou hast planted,
And sweep thence the strangers, and save us now!
O regard the covenant which thou hast sealed in us!
O remember for us the father who knew thee,
To whom thou, too, didst make known thy love,
     And save us now!

O deal wondrously with the pure in heart
That thy providence may be seen of men, and save us
     now!
O lift up Zion's sunken gates from the earth,
Exalt the spot to which our eyes all turn,
     And save us now!

Such hymns won for Kalir popularity, which, however, is now
much on the wane.

* * * * *

BIBLIOGRAPHY

KALIR AND JANNAI.

Graetz.—III, 4.
Translations of Poems in Editions of the Prayer-Book, and
     J.Q.R., VII, p. 460; IX, p. 291.
L.N. Dembitz,—*Jewish Services*, p. 222 *seq.*

CHAPTER VIII

SAADIAH OF FAYUM

Translation of the Bible into Arabic.—Foundation of a Jewish Philosophy of Religion.

Saadiah was born in Fayum (Egypt) in 892, and died in Sura in 942. He was the founder of a new literature. In width of culture he excelled all his Jewish contemporaries. To him Judaism was synonymous with culture, and therefore he endeavored to absorb for Judaism all the literary and scientific tendencies of his day. He created, in the first place, a Jewish philosophy, that is to say, he applied to Jewish theology the philosophical methods of the Arabs. Again, though he vigorously opposed Karaism, he adopted its love of philology, and by his translation of the Bible into Arabic helped forward a sounder understanding of the Scriptures.

At the age of thirty-six Saadiah received a remarkable honor; he was summoned to Sura to fill the post of Gaon. This election of a foreigner as head of the Babylonian school proves, first, that Babylonia had lost its old supremacy, and, secondly, that Saadiah had already won world-wide fame. Yet the great work on which his reputation now rests was not then written. Saadiah's notoriety was due to his successful championship of Rabbinism against the Karaites. His determination, his learning, his originality, were all discernible in his early treatises against Anan and his followers. The Rabbinites had previously opposed Karaism in a guerilla warfare. Saadiah came into the open, and met and vanquished the foe in pitched battles. But he did more than defeat the invader, he strengthened the home defences. Saadiah's polemical works have always a positive as well as a negative value. He wished to prove Karaism wrong, but he also tried to show that Rabbinism was right.

As a champion of Rabbinism, then, Saadiah was called to Sura. But he had another claim to distinction. The Karaites founded their position on the Bible. Saadiah resolved that the appeal to the Bible should not be restricted to scholars. He translated the Scriptures into Arabic, and added notes. Saadiah's qualifications for the task were his knowledge of Hebrew, his fine critical sense, and his enlightened attitude towards the Midrash. As to the first qualification, it is said that at the age of eleven he had begun a Hebrew rhyming dictionary for the use of poets. He himself added several hymns to the liturgy. In these Saadiah's poetical range is very varied. Sometimes his style is as pure and simple as the most classical poems of the Spanish school. At other times, his verses have all the intricacy, harshness, and artificiality of Kalir's. Perhaps his mastery of Hebrew is best seen in his "Book of the Exiled" (*Sefer ha-Galui*), compiled in Biblical Hebrew, divided into verses, and provided with accents. As the title indicates, this book was written during Saadiah's exile from Sura.

Saadiah's Arabic version of the Scriptures won such favor that it was read publicly in the synagogues. Of old the Targum, or Aramaic version, had been read in public worship together with the original Hebrew. Now, however, the Arabic began to replace the Targum. Saadiah's version well deserved its honor.

Saadiah brought a hornet's nest about his head by his renewed attacks on Karaism, contained in his commentary to Genesis. But the call to Sura turned Saadiah's thoughts in another direction. He found the famous college in decay. The Exilarchs, the nominal heads of the whole of the Babylonian Jews, were often unworthy of their position, and it was not long before Saadiah came into conflict with the Exilarch. The struggle ended in the Gaon's exile from Sura. During his years of banishment, he produced his greatest works. He arranged a prayer-book, wrote Talmudical essays, compiled rules for the calendar, examined the Massoretic works of various authors, and, indeed, produced a vast array of books, all of them influential and meritorious. But his most memorable writings were his "Commentary on the Book of Creation" (*Sefer Yetsirah*) and his masterpiece, "Faith and Philosophy" (*Emunoth ve-Deoth*).

This treatise, finished in the year 934, was the first systematic attempt to bring revealed religion into harmony with Greek philosophy. Saadiah was thus the forerunner, not only of Maimonides, but also of the Christian school-men. No Jew, said Saadiah, should discard the Bible, and form his opinions solely by his own reasoning. But he might safely endeavor to prove, independently of revelation, the truths which revelation had given. Faith, said Saadiah again, is the sours absorption of the essence of a truth, which thus becomes part of itself, and will be the motive of conduct whenever the occasion arises. Thus Saadiah identified reason with faith. He ridiculed the fear that philosophy leads to scepticism. You might as well, he argued, identify astronomy with superstition, because some deluded people believe that an eclipse of the moon is caused by a dragon's making a meal of it.

For the last few years of his life Saadiah was reinstated in the Gaonate at Sura. The school enjoyed a new lease of fame under the brilliant direction of the author of the great work just described. After his death the inevitable decay made itself felt. Under the Moorish caliphs, Spain had become a centre of Arabic science, art, and poetry. In the tenth century, Cordova attained fame similar to that which Athens and Alexandria had once reached. In Moorish Spain, there was room both for earnest piety and the sensuous delights of music and art; and the keen exercise of the intellect in science or philosophy did not debar the possession of practical statesmanship and skill in affairs. In the service of the caliphs were politicians who were also doctors, poets, philosophers, men of science. Possession of culture was, indeed, a sure credential for employment by the state. It was to Moorish Spain that the centre of Judaism shifted after the death of Saadiah. It was in Spain that the finest fruit of Jewish literature in the post-Biblical period grew. Here the Jewish genius expanded beneath the sunshine of Moorish culture. To Moses, the son of Chanoch, an envoy from Babylonia, belongs the honor of founding a new school in Cordova. In this he had the support of the scholar-statesman Chasdai, the first of a long line of medieval Jews who earned double fame, as servants of their country and as servants of their own religion. To Chasdai we must now turn.

* * * * *

BIBLIOGRAPHY

SAADIAH.

Graetz.—III, 7.

Schiller-Szinessy.—*Encycl. Brit.*, Vol. XXI, p. 120.

M. Friedländer.—*Life and Works of Saadia. J.Q.R.*, Vol. V, p. 177.

Saadiah's Philosophy (Owen), *J.Q.R.*, Vol. III, p. 192.

Grammar and Polemics (Rosin), *J.Q.R.*, Vol. VI, p. 475; (S. Poznanski) *ibid.*, Vol. IX, p. 238.

E.H. Lindo.—*History of the Jews of Spain and Portugal* (London, 1848).

CHAPTER IX

DAWN OF THE SPANISH ERA

Chasdai Ibn Shaprut.—Menachem and Dunash, Chayuj and Janach.—Samuel the Nagid.

If but a small part of what Hebrew poets sang concerning Chasdai Ibn Shaprut be literal fact, he was indeed a wonderful figure. His career set the Jewish imagination aflame. Charizi, in the thirteenth century, wrote of Chasdai thus:

> In southern Spain, in days gone by,
> The sun of fame rose up on high:
> Chasdai it was, the prince, who gave
> Rich gifts to all who came to crave.
> Science rolled forth her mighty waves,
> Laden with gems from hidden caves,
> Till wisdom like an island stood,
> The precious outcome of the flood.
> Here thirsting spirits still might find
> Knowledge to satisfy the mind.
> Their prince's favor made new day
> For those who slept their life away.
> They who had lived so long apart
> Confessed a bond, a common heart,
> From Christendom and Moorish lands,
> From East, from West, from distant strands.
> His favor compassed each and all.
> Girt by the shelter of his grace,
> Lit by the glory of his face,
> Knowledge held their heart in thrall.

He showed the source of wisdom and her springs,
And God's anointment made them more than kings.
His goodness made the dumb to speak his name,
Yea, stubborn hearts were not unyielding long;
And bards the starry splendor of his fame
Mirrored in lucent current of their song.

This Chasdai, the son of Isaac, of the family of Shaprut (915-970), was a physician and a statesman. He was something of a poet and linguist besides; not much of a poet, for his eulogists say little of his verses; and not much of a linguist, for he employed others (among them Menachem, the son of Zaruk, the grammarian) to write his Hebrew letters for him. But he was enough of a scholar to appreciate learning in others, and as a patron of literature he placed himself in the front of the new Jewish development in Spain. From Babylonia he was hailed as the head of the school in Cordova. At his palatial abode was gathered all that was best in Spanish Judaism. He was the patron of the two great grammarians of the day, Menachem, the son of Zaruk, and his rival and critic, Dunash, the son of Labrat. These grammarians fought out their literary disputes in verses dedicated to Chasdai. Witty satires were written by the friends of both sides. Sparkling epigrams were exchanged in the rose-garden of Chasdai's house, and were read at the evening assemblies of poets, merchants, and courtiers. It was Chasdai who brought both the rivals to Cordova, Menachem from Tortosa and Dunash from Fez. Menachem was the founder of scientific Hebrew grammar; Dunash, more lively but less scholarly, initiated the art of writing metrical Hebrew verses. The successors of these grammarians, Judah Chayuj and Abulwalid Merwan Ibn Janach (eleventh century), completed what Menachem and Dunash had begun, and placed Hebrew philology on a firm scientific basis.

Thus, with Chasdai a new literary era dawned for Judaism. His person, his glorious position, his liberal encouragement of poetry and learning, opened the sealed-up lips of the Hebrew muse. As a contemporary said of Chasdai:

The grinding yoke from Israel's neck he tore,
Deep in his soul his people's love he bore.
The sword that thirsted for their blood he brake,

And cold oppression melted for his sake.
For God sent Chasdai Israel's heart to move
Once more to trust, once more his God to love.

Chasdai did not confine his efforts on behalf of his brethren
to the Jews of Spain. Ambition and sympathy made him extend his
affection to the Jews of all the world. He interviewed the captains
of ships, he conversed with foreign envoys concerning the Jews of
other lands. He entered into a correspondence with the Chazars,
Jews by adoption, not by race. It is not surprising that the influence
of Chasdai survived him. Under the next two caliphs, Cordova
continued the centre of a cultured life and literature. Thither
flocked, not only the Chazars, but also the descendants of the
Babylonian Princes of the Captivity and other men of note.

Half a century after Chasdai's death, Samuel Ibn Nagdela
(993-1055) stood at the head of the Jewish community in Granada.
Samuel, called the Nagid, or Prince, started life as a druggist in
Malaga. His fine handwriting came to the notice of the vizier, and
Samuel was appointed private secretary. His talents as a statesman
were soon discovered, and he was made first minister to Habus,
the ruler of Granada. Once a Moor insulted him, and King Habus
advised his favorite to cut out the offender's tongue. But Samuel
treated his reviler with much kindness, and one day King Habus
and Samuel passed the same Moor. "He blesses you now," said the
astonished king, "whom he used to curse."

"Ah!" replied Samuel, "I did as you advised. I cut out his angry
tongue, and put a kind one there instead."

Samuel was not only vizier, he was also Rabbi. His knowledge
of the Rabbinical literature was profound, and his "Introduction to
the Talmud" (*Mebo ha-Talmud*) is still a standard work. He expended
much labor and money on collecting the works of the Gaonim.
The versatility of Samuel was extraordinary. From the palace he
would go to the school; after inditing a despatch he would compose
a hymn; he would leave a reception of foreign diplomatists to
discuss intricate points of Rabbinical law or examine the latest
scientific discoveries. As a poet, his muse was that of the town, not
of the field. But though he wrote no nature poems, he resembled
the ancient Hebrew Psalmists in one striking feature. He sang new
songs of thanksgiving over his own triumphs, uttered laments on his

own woes, but there is an impersonal note in these songs as there is in the similar lyrics of the Psalter. His individual triumphs and woes were merged in the triumphs and woes of his people. In all, Samuel added some thirty new hymns to the liturgy of the Synagogue. But his muse was as versatile as his mind. Samuel also wrote some stirring wine songs. The marvellous range of his powers helped him to complete what Chasdai had begun. The centre of Judaism became more firmly fixed than ever in Spain. When Samuel the Nagid died in 1055, the golden age of Spanish literature was in sight. Above the horizon were rising in a glorious constellation, Solomon Ibn Gebirol, the Ibn Ezras, and Jehuda Halevi.

* * * * *

BIBLIOGRAPHY

CHASDAI.

Graetz,—III, p. 215 [220].

DUNASH AND MENACHEM.

Graetz.—III, p. 223 [228].

JANACH.

Encycl. Brit., Vol. XIII, p. 737.

CHAYUJ.

M. Jastrow, Jr.—*The Weak and Geminative Verbs in Hebrew by Hayyûg* (Leyden, 1897).

HEBREW PHILOLOGY.

Steinschneider.—*Jewish Literature*, p. 131.

CHAZARS.

Letter of Chasdai to Chazars (Engl. transl. by Zedner, *Miscellany of the Society of Hebrew Literature*, Vol. I).
Graetz.—III, p. 138 [140].

SAMUEL IBN NAGDELA.

Graetz,—III, p, 254 [260].

CHAPTER X

THE SPANISH-JEWISH POETS (I)

Solomon Ibn Gebirol.—"The Royal Crown."—Moses Ibn Ezra.—
Abraham Ibn Ezra.—The Biblical Commentaries of Ibn Ezra and
the Kimchis.

"In the days of Chasdai," says Charizi, "the Hebrew poets
began to sing." We have seen that the new-Hebrew poetry was older
than Chasdai, but Charizi's assertion is true. The Hebrew poets of
Spain are melodious, and Kalir is only ingenious. Again, it was in
Spain that Hebrew was first used for secular poetry, for love songs
and ballads, for praises of nature, for the expression of all human
feelings. In most of this the poets found their models in the Bible.
When Jehuda Halevi sang in Hebrew of love, he echoed the "Song
of Songs." When Moses Ibn Ezra wrote penitential hymns, or Ibn
Gebirol divine meditations, the Psalms were ever before them as an
inspiration. The poets often devoted all their ambition to finding
apt quotations from the sacred text. But in one respect they failed
to imitate the Bible, and this failure seriously cramped their genius.
The poetry of the Bible depends for its beauty partly on its form.
This form is what is called *parallelism of line*. The fine musical effect
produced by repeating as an echo the idea already expressed is lost
in the poetry of the Spanish Jews.

Thus Spanish-Jewish poetry suffers, on the one side, because
it is an imitation of the Bible, and therefore lacks originality, and
on the other side it suffers, because it does not sufficiently imitate
the Biblical style. In spite of these limitations, it is real poetry. In
the Psalms there is deep sympathy for the wilder and more awful

phenomena of nature. In the poetry of the Spanish Jews, nature is loved in her gentler moods. One of these poets, Nahum, wrote prettily of his garden; another, Ibn Gebirol, sang of autumn; Jehuda Halevi, of spring. Again, in their love songs there is freshness. There is in them a quaint blending of piety and love; they do not say that beauty is a vain thing, but they make beauty the mark of a God-fearing character. There is an un-Biblical lightness of touch, too, in their songs of life in the city, their epigrams, their society verses. And in those of their verses which most resemble the Bible, the passionate odes to Zion by Jehuda Halevi, the sublime meditations of Ibn Gebirol, the penitential prayers of Moses Ibn Ezra, though the echoes of the Bible are distinct enough, yet amid the echoes there sounds now and again the fresh, clear voice of the medieval poet.

Solomon Ibn Gebirol was born in Malaga in 1021, and died in 1070. His early life was unhappy, and his poetry is tinged with melancholy. But his unhappiness only gave him a fuller hope in God. As he writes in his greatest poem, he would fly from God to God:

> From thee to thee I fly to win
> A place of refuge, and within
> Thy shadow from thy anger hide,
> Until thy wrath be turned aside.
> Unto thy mercy I will cling,
> Until thou hearken pitying;
> Nor will I quit my hold of thee,
> Until thy blessing light on me.

These lines occur in Gebirol's "Royal Crown" (*Kether Malchuth*) a glorious series of poems on God and the world. In this, the poet pours forth his heart even more unreservedly than in his philosophical treatise, "The Fountain of Life," or in his ethical work, "The Ennoblement of Character," or in his compilation from the wisdom of the past, "The Choice of Pearls" (if, indeed, this last book be his). The "Royal Crown" is a diadem of praises of the greatness of God, praises to utter which make man, with all his insignificance, great.

Wondrous are thy works, O Lord of hosts,
And their greatness holds my soul in thrall.
Thine the glory is, the power divine,
Thine the majesty, the kingdom thine,
Thou supreme, exalted over all.

* * * *

Thou art One, the first great cause of all;
Thou art One, and none can penetrate,
Not even the wise in heart, the mystery
Of thy unfathomable Unity;
Thou art One, the infinitely great.

But man can perceive that the power of God makes him great to pardon. If he see it not now, he will hereafter.

Thou art light: pure souls shall thee behold,
Save when mists of evil intervene.
Thou art light, that, in this world concealed,
In the world to come shall be revealed;
In the mount of God it shall be seen.

And so the poet in one of the final hymns of the "Royal Crown," filled with a sense of his own unworthiness, hopefully abandons himself to God:

My God, I know that those who plead
To thee for grace and mercy need
All their good works should go before,
And wait for them at heaven's high door.
But no good deeds have I to bring,
No righteousness for offering.
No service for my Lord and King.

Yet hide not thou thy face from me,
Nor cast me out afar from thee;
But when thou bidd'st my life to cease,
ou lead me forth in peace
Unto the world to come, to dwell

Among thy pious ones, who tell
Thy glories inexhaustible.

There let my portion be with those
Who to eternal life arose;
There purify my heart aright,
In thy light to behold the light.
Raise me from deepest depths to share
Heaven's endless joys of praise and prayer,
That I may evermore declare:
Though thou wast angered, Lord, I will give thanks to
    thee,
For past is now thy wrath, and thou dost comfort me.

Ibn Gebirol stood a little outside and a good deal above the
circle of the Jewish poets who made this era so brilliant. Many of
them are now forgotten; they had their day of popularity in Toledo,
Cordova, Seville, and Granada, but their poems have not survived.

In the very year of Ibn Gebirol's death Moses Ibn Ezra was
born. Of his life little is certain, but it is known that he was still
alive in 1138. He is called the "poet of penitence," and a gloomy
turn was given to his thought by an unhappy love attachment in his
youth. A few stanzas of one of his poems run thus:

Sleepless, upon my bed the hours I number,
And, rising, seek the house of God, while slumber
Lies heavy on men's eyes, and dreams encumber
Their souls in visions of the night.

In sin and folly passed my early years,
Wherefore I am ashamed, and life's arrears
Now strive to pay, the while my tears
Have been my food by day and night.

* * * * *

Short is man's life, and full of care and sorrow,
This way and that he turns some ease to borrow,
Like to a flower he blooms, and on the morrow
Is gone—a vision of the night.

How does the weight of sin my soul oppress,
Because God's law too often I transgress;
I mourn and sigh, with tears of bitterness
My bed I water all the night.

* * * * *

My youth wanes like a shadow that's cast,
Swifter than eagle's wings my years fly fast,
And I remember not my gladness past,
Either by day or yet by night.

Proclaim we then a fast, a holy day,
Make pure our hearts from sin, God's will obey,
And unto him, with humbled spirit pray
Unceasingly, by day and night.

May we yet hear his words: "Thou art my own,
My grace is thine, the shelter of my throne,
For I am thy Redeemer, I alone;
Endure but patiently this night!"

But his hymns, many of which won a permanent place in the prayer-book, are not always sad. Often they are warm with hope, and there is a lilt about them which is almost gay. His chief secular poem, "The Topaz" (*Tarshish*), is in ten parts, and contains 1210 lines. It is written on an Arabic model: it contains no rhymes, but is metrical, and the same word, with entirely different meanings, occurs at the end of several lines. It needs a good deal of imagination to appreciate Moses Ibn Ezra, and this is perhaps what Charizi meant when he called him "the poet's poet."

Another Ibn Ezra, Abraham, one of the greatest Jews of the Middle Ages, was born in Toledo before 1100. He passed a hard life, but he laughed at his fate. He said of himself:

If I sold shrouds,
        No one would die.
If I sold lamps,
        Then, in the sky,
The sun, for spite,
Would shine by night.

Several of Abraham Ibn Ezra's hymns are instinct with the spirit of resignation. Here is one of them:

> I hope for the salvation of the Lord,
> In him I trust, when fears my being thrill,
> Come life, come death, according to his word,
> He is my portion still.
>
> Hence, doubting heart! I will the Lord extol
> With gladness, for in him is my desire,
> Which, as with fatness, satisfies my soul,
> That doth to heaven aspire.
>
> All that is hidden shall mine eyes behold,
> And the great Lord of all be known to me,
> Him will I serve, his am I as of old;
> I ask not to be free.
>
> Sweet is ev'n sorrow coming in his name,
> Nor will I seek its purpose to explore,
> His praise will I continually proclaim,
> And bless him evermore.

Ibn Ezra wandered over many lands, and even visited London, where he stayed in 1158. Ibn Ezra was famed, not only for his poetry, but also for his brilliant wit and many-sided learning. As a mathematician, as a poet, as an expounder of Scriptures, he won a high place in Jewish annals. In his commentaries he rejected the current digressive and allegorical methods, and steered a middle course between free research on the one hand, and blind adherence to tradition on the other. Ibn Ezra was the first to maintain that the Book of Isaiah contains the work of two prophets—a view now almost universal. He never for a moment doubted, however, that the Bible was in every part inspired and in every part the word of God. But he was also the father of the "Higher Criticism." Ibn Ezra's pioneer work in spreading scientific methods of study in France was shared by Joseph Kimchi, who settled in Narbonne in the middle of the twelfth century. His sons, Moses and David, were afterwards famous as grammarians and interpreters of the Scriptures. David Kimchi (1160-1235) by his lucidity and thoroughness established for his grammar, "Perfection" (*Michlol*), and his dictionary, "Book of Roots," complete supremacy in the field of exegesis. He was the favorite authority of the Christian students of Hebrew at the time of the Reformation, and the English Authorized Version of 1611 owed much to him.

At this point, however, we must retrace our steps, and cast a glance at Hebrew literature in France at a period earlier than the era of Ibn Ezra.

* * * * *

BIBLIOGRAPHY

TRANSLATIONS OF SPANISH-HEBREW POEMS:

> Emma Lazarus.—*Poems* (Boston, 1889).
> Mrs. H. Lucas.—*The Jewish Year* (New York, 1898), and in Editions of the Prayer-Books. See also (Abrahams) *J.Q.R.*, XI, p. 64.

IBN GEBIROL.

> Graetz.—III, 9.
> D. Rosin.—*The Ethics of Solomon Ibn Gebirol*, 7. *J.Q.R.*, III, p. 159.

MOSES IBN EZRA.

> Graetz.—III, p. 319 [326].

ABRAHAM IBN EZRA.

> Graetz.—III, p. 366 [375].
> Abraham Ibn Ezra's Commentary on Isaiah (tr. by M. Friedländer, 1873).
> M. Friedländer.—*Essays on Ibn Ezra* (London, 1877). See also *Transactions of the Jewish Historical Society of England*, Vol. II, p. 47, and J. Jacobs, *Jews of Angevin England*, p. 29 *seq.*

KIMCHI FAMILY.

> Graetz.—III, p. 392 [404].

SPANISH-JEWISH EXEGESIS AND POETRY.

> Steinschneider.—*Jewish Literature*, pp. 141, 146-179.

CHAPTER XI

RASHI AND ALFASSI

Nathan of Rome.—Alfassi.—Rashi.—Rashbam.

Before Hebrew poets, scientists, philosophers, and statesmen had made Spain famous in Jewish annals, Rashi and his school were building up a reputation destined to associate Jewish learning with France. In France there was none of the width of culture which distinguished Spain. Rashi did not shine as anything but an exponent of traditional Judaism. He possessed no graces of style, created no new literature. But he represented Judaism at its simplest, its warmest, its intensest. Rashi was a great writer because his subject was great, not because he wrote greatly.

But it is only a half-truth to assert that Rashi had no graces of style. For, if grace be the quality of producing effects with the least display of effort, then there was no writer more graceful than Rashi. His famous Commentary on the Talmud is necessarily long and intricate, but there is never a word too much. No commentator on any classic ever surpassed Rashi in the power of saying enough and only enough. He owed this faculty in the first place to his intellectual grasp. He edited the Talmud as well as explained it. He restored the original text with the surest of critical instincts. And his conscience was in his work. So thoroughly honest was he that, instead of slurring over difficulties, he frankly said: "I cannot understand . . . I do not know," in the rare cases in which he was at a loss. Rashi moreover possessed that wondrous sympathy with author and reader which alone qualifies a third mind to interpret author to reader. Probing the depth of the Talmud, Rashi probed the depth of the learned student, and realized the needs of the beginner. Thus the beginner finds Rashi useful, and the specialist turns to him for help. His immediate disciples rarely quote him by name; to them he is "*the* Commentator."

Rashi was not the first to subject the Talmud to critical analysis. The Gaonim had begun the task, and Nathan, the son of Yechiel of Rome, compiled, in about the year 1000, a dictionary (*Aruch*) which is still the standard work of reference. But Rashi's nearest predecessor, Alfassi, was not an expounder of the Talmud; he extracted, with much skill, the practical results from the logical mazes in which they were enveloped. Isaac, the son of Jacob Alfassi, derived his name from Fez, where he was born in 1013. He gave his intellect entirely to the Talmud, but he acquired from the Moorish culture of his day a sense of order and system. He dealt exclusively with the *Halachah*, or practical contents of the Rabbinic law, and the guide which he compiled to the Talmud soon superseded all previous works of its kind. Solomon, the son of Isaac, best known as Rabbi *Sh*elomo *Iz*chaki (Rashi), was born in 1040, and died in 1105, in Troyes, in Champagne. From his mother, who came of a family of poets, he inherited his warm humanity, his love for Judaism. From his father, he drew his Talmudical knowledge, his keen intellect. His youth was a hard one. In accordance with medieval custom, he was married as a boy, and then left his home in search of knowledge rather than of bread. Of bread he had little, but, starved and straitened in circumstances though he was, he became an eager student at the Jewish schools which then were dotted along the Rhine, residing now at Mainz, now at Speyer, now at Worms. In 1064 he settled finally in Troyes. Here he was at once hailed as a new light in Israel. His spotless character and his unique reputation as a teacher attracted a vast number of eager students.

Of Rashi's Commentary on the Talmud something has already been said. As to his exposition of the Bible, it soon acquired the widest popularity. It was inferior to his work on the Talmud, for, as he himself admitted in later life, he had relied too much on the Midrash, and had attended too little to evolving the literal meaning of the text of Scripture. But this is the charm of his book, and it is fortunate that he did not actually attempt to recast his commentary. There is a quaintness and fascination about it which are lacking in the pedantic sobriety of Ibn Ezra and the grammatical exactness of

Kimchi. But he did himself less than justice when he asserted that he had given insufficient heed to the *Peshat* (literal meaning). Rashi often quotes the grammatical works of Menachem and Dunash. He often translates the Hebrew into French, showing a very exact knowledge of both languages. Besides, when he cites the Midrash, he, as it were, constructs a Peshat out of it, and this method, original to himself, found no capable imitators.

Through the fame of Rashi, France took the leadership in matters Talmudical. Blessed with a progeny of famous men, Rashi's influence was carried on and increased by the work of his sons-in-law and grandsons. Of these, Samuel ben Meir (Rashbam, 1100-1160) was the most renowned. The devoted attention to the literature of Judaism in the Rhinelands came in the nick of time. It was a firm rock against the storm which was about to break. The Crusades crushed out from the Jews of France all hope of temporal happiness. When Alfassi died in 1103 and Rashi in 1105, the first Crusade had barely spent its force. The Jewish schools in France were destroyed, the teachers and scholars massacred or exiled. But the spirit lived on. Their literature was life to the Jews, who had no other life. His body bent over Rashi's illuminating expositions of the Talmud and the Bible, the medieval Jew felt his soul raised above the miseries of the present to a world of peace and righteousness, where the wicked ceased from troubling, and the weary were at rest.

* * * * *

BIBLIOGRAPHY

ALFASSI AND RASHI.

Graetz.—III, p. 285 [292] *seq.*

ALFASSI.

I.H. Weiss.—*J.Q.R.*, I, p. 290.

RASHI.

Schiller-Szinessy.—*Encycl. Brit.*, Vol. XX, p. 284.

CHAPTER XII

THE SPANISH-JEWISH POETS (II)

Jehuda Halevi.—Charizi.

Turning once more to the brighter condition of Jewish literature in Spain, we reach a man upon whom the whole vocabulary of praise and affection has been exhausted; a man of magnetic attractiveness, whom contemporaries and successors have agreed to admire and to love. Jehuda Halevi was born in Toledo about 1085, the year in which Alfonso VI recaptured the city from the Moors. It was a fit birth-place for the greatest Jewish poet since Bible times. East and West met in Toledo. The science of the East there found Western Christians to cultivate it. Jew, Moor, and Christian displayed there mutual toleration which existed nowhere else. In the midst of this favorable environment Jehuda Halevi grew to early maturity. As a boy he won more than local fame as a versifier. At all festive occasions his verses were in demand. He wrote wedding odes, elegies on great men, eulogies of the living. His love poems, serenades, epigrams of this period, all display taste, elegance, and passion.

The second period of Jehuda Halevi's literary career was devoted to serious pursuits, to thoughts about life, and to practical work. He wrote his far-famed philosophical dialogue, the *Cuzari*, and earned his living as a physician. He was not an enthusiastic devotee to medicine, however. "Toledo is large," he wrote to a friend, "and my patients are hard masters. I, their slave, spend my days in serving their will, and consume my years in healing their infirmities." Before making up a prescription, he, like Sir Thomas

Browne, used to say a prayer in which he confessed that he had no great faith in the healing powers of his art. Jehuda Halevi was, indeed, dissatisfied with his life altogether. "My heart is in the East, but I am sunk in the West," he lamented. He was unhappy because his beloved was far from him; his lady-love was beyond the reach of his earnest gaze. In Heine's oft-quoted words,

> She for whom the Rabbi languished
> Was a woe-begone poor darling,
> Desolation's very image,
> And her name—Jerusalem.

The eager passion for one sight of Jerusalem grew on him, and dominated the third portion of his life. At length nothing could restrain him; go he would, though he die in the effort. And go he did, and die he did in the effort. The news of his determination spread through Spain, and everywhere hands were held out to restrain him. But his heart lightened as the day of departure came. His poems written at this time are hopeful and full of cheery feeling. In Egypt, a determined attempt was made by the Jews to keep him among them. But it was vain. Onward to Jerusalem: this was his one thought. He tarried in Egypt but a short while, then he passed to Tyre and Damascus. At Damascus, in the year 1140 or thereabouts, he wrote the ode to Zion which made his name immortal, an ode in which he gave vent to all the intense passion which filled his soul. The following are some stanzas taken from this address to Jerusalem:

> The glory of the Lord has been alway
> Thy sole and perfect light;
> Thou needest not the sun to shine by day,
> Nor moon and stars to illumine thee by night.
> I would that, where God's spirit was of yore
> Poured out unto thy holy ones, I might
> There too my soul outpour!
> The house of kings and throne of God wert thou,
> How comes it then that now
> Slaves fill the throne where sat thy kings before?

Oh! who will lead me on
To seek the spots where, in far distant years,
The angels in their glory dawned upon
Thy messengers and seers?

Oh! who will give me wings
That I may fly away,
And there, at rest from all my wanderings,
The ruins of my heart among thy ruins lay?

* * * * *

The Lord desires thee for his dwelling-place
Eternally, and bless'd
Is he whom God has chosen for the grace
Within thy courts to rest.
Happy is he that watches, drawing near,
Until he sees thy glorious lights arise,
And over whom thy dawn breaks full and clear
Set in the orient skies.
But happiest he, who, with exultant eyes,
The bliss of thy redeemed ones shall behold,
And see thy youth renewed as in the days of old.

Soon after writing this Jehuda arrived near the Holy City. He was by her side at last, by the side of his beloved. Then, legend tells us, through a gate an Arab horseman dashed forth: he raised his spear, and slew the poet, who fell at the threshold of his dear Jerusalem, with a song of Zion on his lips.

The new-Hebrew poetry did not survive him. Persecution froze the current of the Jewish soul. Poets, indeed, arose after Jehuda Halevi in Germany as in Spain. Sometimes, as in the hymns of the "German" Meir of Rothenburg, a high level of passionate piety is reached. But it has well been said that "the hymns of the Spanish writers link man's soul to his Maker: the hymns of the Germans link Israel to his God." Only in Spain Hebrew poetry was universal, in the sense in which the Psalms are universal. Even in Spain itself, the death of Jehuda Halevi marked the close of this higher inspiration. The later Spanish poets, Charizi and Zabara (middle and end of the twelfth century), were satirists rather than poets, witty, sparkling, ready with quaint quips, but local and imitative in manner and subject. Zabara must receive some further notice in a later chapter because of his connection with medieval folk-lore. Of Charizi's chief work, the *Tachkemoni*, it may be said that it is excellent of its type. The stories which it tells in unmetrical rhyme are told in racy style, and its criticisms on men and things are clever and striking. As a literary critic also Charizi ranks high, and there is much skill in the manner in which he links together, round the person of his hero, the various narratives which compose the *Tachkemoni*. The experiences he relates are full of humor and surprises. As a phrase-maker, Charizi was peculiarly happy, his command of Hebrew being masterly. But his most conspicuous claim to high rank lies in his origination of that blending of grim irony with bright wit which became characteristic of all Jewish humorists, and reached its climax in Heine. But Charizi himself felt that his art as a Hebrew poet was decadent. Great poets of Jewish race have risen since, but the songs they have sung have not been songs of Zion, and the language of their muse has not been the language of the Hebrew Bible.

* * * * *

BIBLIOGRAPHY

JEHUDA HALEVI.

>   Graetz.—III, II.
>   J. Jacobs.—*Jehuda Halevi, Poet and Pilgrim (Jewish Ideals*, New
>   York, 1896, p. 103).
>   Lady Magnus.—*Jewish Portraits* (Boston, 1889), p. 1.

TRANSLATIONS OF HIS POETRY by Emma Lazarus and Mrs. Lucas (*op. cit.*): Editions of the Prayer-Book; also *J.Q.R.*, X, pp. 117, 626; VII, p. 464;

>   *Treasurers of Oxford* (London, 1850); I. Abrahams, *Jewish Life in
>   the Middle Ages*, chs. 7, 9 and 10.

HIS PHILOSOPHY: *Specimen of the Cusari*, translated by A. Neubauer (*Miscellany of the Society of Hebrew Literature*, Vol. I).

John Owen.—*J.Q.R.*, III, p. 199.

CHARIZI.

Graetz.—III, p. 559 [577]
Karpeles.—*Jewish Literature and other Essays*, p. 210 *seq.*
M. Sachs.—*Hebrew Review*, Vol. I.

CHAPTER XIII

MOSES MAIMONIDES

Maimon, Rambam = R. Moses, the son of Maimon, Maimonides.—
His Yad Hachazaka and Moreh Nebuchim.—Gersonides.—
Crescas.—Albo.

The greatest Jew of the Middle Ages, Moses, the son of
Maimon, was born in Cordova, in 1135, and died in Fostat in 1204.
His father Maimon was himself an accomplished scientist and an
enlightened thinker, and the son was trained in the many arts and
sciences then included in a liberal education. When Moses was
thirteen years old, Cordova fell into the hands of the Almohades, a
sect of Mohammedans, whose creed was as pure as their conduct
was fanatical. Jews and Christians were forced to choose conversion
to Islam, exile, or death. Maimon fled with his family, and, after an
interval of troubled wanderings and painful privations, they settled
in Fez, where they found the Almohades equally powerful and
equally vindictive. Maimon and his son were compelled to assume
the outward garb of Mohammedanism for a period of five years.
From Fez the family emigrated in 1165 to Palestine, and, after a
long period of anxiety, Moses Maimonides settled in Egypt, in
Fostat, or Old Cairo.

In Egypt, another son of Maimon, David, traded in precious
stones, and supported his learned brother. When David was lost at
sea, Maimonides earned a living as a physician. His whole day was
occupied in his profession, yet he contrived to work at his books
during the greater part of the night. His minor works would alone
have brought their author fame. His first great work was completed

in 1168. It was a Commentary on the Mishnah, and was written in Arabic. But Maimonides' reputation rests mainly on two books, the one written for the many, the other for the few. The former is his "Strong Hand" (*Yad Hachazaka*), the latter his "Guide of the Perplexed" (*Moreh Nebuchim*).

The "Strong Hand" was a gigantic undertaking. In its fourteen books Maimonides presented a clearly-arranged and clearly-worded summary of the Rabbinical Halachah, or Law. In one sense it is an encyclopedia, but it is an encyclopedia written with style. For its power to grapple with vast materials, this code has few rivals and no superiors in other literatures. Maimonides completed its compilation in 1180, having spent ten years over it. During the whole of that time, he was not only a popular doctor, but also official Rabbi of Cairo. He received no salary from the community, for he said, "Better one penny earned by the work of one's hands, than all the revenues of the Prince of the Captivity, if derived from fees for teaching or acting as Rabbi." The "Strong Hand," called also "Deuteronomy" (*Mishneh Torah*), sealed the reputation of Maimonides for all time. Maimonides was indeed attacked, first, because he asserted that his work was intended to make a study of the Talmud less necessary, and secondly, because he gave no authorities for his statements, but decided for himself which Talmudical opinions to accept, which to reject. But the severest scrutiny found few real blemishes and fewer actual mistakes. "From Moses to Moses there arose none like Moses," was a saying that expressed the general reverence for Maimonides. Copies of the book were made everywhere; the Jewish mind became absorbed in it; his fame and his name "rang from Spain to India, from the sources of the Tigris to South Arabia." Eulogies were showered on him from all parts of the earth. And no praise can say more for this marvellous man than the fact that the incense burned at his shrine did not intoxicate him. His touch became firmer, his step more resolute. But he went on his way as before, living simply and laboring incessantly, unmoved by the thunders of applause, unaffected by the feebler echoes of calumny. He corresponded with his brethren far and near, answered questions as Rabbi, explained passages in his Commentary on the Mishnah or his other writings, entered heartily into the controversies of the day, discussed the claims of a new aspirant to the dignity of Messiah, encouraged the weaker brethren who fell under disfavor because they had been compelled to become pretended converts to Islam, showed common-sense and strong intellectual grasp in every line he wrote, and combined in his dealings with all questions the rarely associated qualities, toleration and devotion to the truth. Yet he felt that his life's work was still incomplete. He loved truth, but truth for him had two aspects: there was truth as revealed by God, there was truth which God left man to discover for himself. In the mind of Maimonides, Moses and Aristotle occupied pedestals side by side. In the "Strong Hand," he had codified and given orderly arrangement to Judaism as revealed in Bible and tradition; he would now examine its relations to reason, would compare its results with the data of philosophy. This he did in his "Guide of the Perplexed" (*Moreh Nebuchim*). Maimonides here differed fundamentally from his immediate predecessors. Jehuda Halevi, in his *Cuzari*, was poet more than philosopher. The *Cuzari* was a dialogue based on the three principles, that God is revealed in history, that Jerusalem is the centre of the world, and that Israel is to the nations as the heart to the limbs. Jehuda Halevi supported these ideas with arguments deduced from the philosophy of his day, he used reason as the handmaid of theology. Maimonides, however, like Saadiah, recognized a higher function for reason. He placed reason on the same level as revelation, and then demonstrated that his faith and his reason taught identical truths. His work, the "Guide of the Perplexed," written in Arabic in about the year 1190, is based, on the one hand, on the Aristotelian system as expounded by Arabian thinkers, and, on the other hand, on a firm belief in Scripture and tradition. With a masterly hand, Maimonides summarized the teachings of Aristotle and the doctrines of Moses and the Rabbis. Between these two independent bodies of truths he found, not contradiction, but agreement, and he reconciled them in a way that satisfied so many minds that the "Guide" was translated into Hebrew twice during his life-time, and was studied by Mohammedans and by Christians such as Thomas Aquinas. With general readers, the third part was the most popular. In this part Maimonides offered rational explanations of the ceremonial and legislative details of the Bible.

For a long time after the death of Maimonides, which took place in 1204, Jewish thought found in the "Guide" a strong attraction or a violent repulsion. Commentaries on the *Moreh*, or "Guide," multiplied apace. Among the most original of the philosophical successors of Maimonides there were few Jews but were greatly influenced by him. Even the famous author of "The Wars of the Lord," Ralbag, Levi, the son of Gershon (Gersonides), who was born in 1288, and died in 1344, was more or less at the same stand-point as Maimonides. On the other hand, Chasdai Crescas, in his "Light of God," written between 1405 and 1410, made a determined attack on Aristotle, and dealt a serious blow at Maimonides. Crescas' work influenced the thought of Spinoza, who was also a close student of Maimonides. A pupil of Crescas, Joseph Albo (1380-1444) was likewise a critic of Maimonides. Albo's treatise, "The Book of Principles" (*Ikkarim*), became a popular text-book. It was impossible that the reconciliation of Aristotle and Moses should continue to satisfy Jewish readers, when Aristotle had been dethroned from his position of dictator in European thought. But the "Guide" of Maimonides was a great achievement for its spirit more than for its contents. If it inevitably became obsolete as a system of theology, it permanently acted as an antidote to the mysticism which in the thirteenth century began to gain a hold on Judaism, and which, but for Maimonides, might have completely undermined the beliefs of the Synagogue. Maimonides remained the exemplar of reasoning faith long after his particular form of reasoning had become unacceptable to the faithful.

* * * * *

BIBLIOGRAPHY

MAIMONIDES.

Graetz.—III, 14.
Karpeles.—*Jewish Literature and other Essays*, p. 145.
Steinschneider.—*Jewish Literature*, pp. 70, 82 *seq.*, 94 *seq.*
Schiller-Szinessy.—*Encycl. Brit.*, Vol. XV, p. 295.

HIS WORKS:

Eight Chapters.—B. Spiers in *Threefold Cord* (1893). English translation in *Hebrew Review*, Vols. I and II.

Strong Hand, selections translated by Soloweycik (London, 1863).

Letter to Jehuda Ibn Tibbon, translated by H. Adler (*Miscellany of the Society of Hebrew Literature*, Vol. I).

Guide of the Perplexed, translated by M. Friedländer (1885).

CRITICAL ESSAYS ON MAIMONIDES:

I.H. Weiss.—*Study of the Talmud in the Thirteenth Century*, J.Q.R., I, p. 290.

J. Owen.—*J.Q.R.*, III, p. 203.

S. Schechter.—*Studies in Judaism*, p. 161 [197], etc.

ON MAIMON (father of Maimonides), see L.M. Simmons, *Letter of Consolation of Maimon ben Joseph*, J.Q.R., II, p. 62.

CRESCAS.

Graetz.—IV, pp. 146 [157], 191 [206].

ALBO.

Graetz.—IV, 7.

English translation of *Ikkarim, Hebrew Review*, Vols. I, II, III.

CHAPTER XIV

THE DIFFUSION OF SCIENCE

Provençal Translators.—The Ibn Tibbons.—Italian Translators.—
Jacob Anatoli.—Kalonymos.—Scientific Literature.

Translators act as mediators between various peoples and ages. They bring the books and ideas of one form of civilization to the minds and hearts of another. In the Middle Ages translations were of more importance than now, since fewer educated people could read foreign languages.

No men of letters were more active than the Jews in this work of diffusion. Dr. Steinschneider fills 1100 large pages with an account of the translations made by Jews in the Middle Ages. Jews co-operated with Mohammedans in making translations from the Greek, as later on they were associated with Christians in making Latin translations of the masterpieces of Greek literature. Most of the Jewish translations, however, that influenced Europe were made from the Arabic into the Hebrew. But though the language of these translations was mostly Hebrew, they were serviceable to others besides Jews. For the Hebrew versions were often only a stage in a longer journey. Sometimes by Jews directly, sometimes by Christian scholars acting in conjunction with Jews, these Hebrew versions were turned into Latin, which most scholars understood, and from the Latin further translations were made into the every-day languages of Europe.

The works so translated were chiefly the scientific and philosophical masterpieces of the Greeks and Arabs. Poetry and history were less frequently the subject of translation, but, as will be seen later on, the spread of the fables of Greece and of the folk-tales of India owed something to Hebrew translators and editors.

Provence was a meeting-place for Arab science and Jewish learning in the Middle Ages, and it was there that the translating impulse of the Jews first showed itself strongly. By the beginning of the thirteenth century, Hebrew translation had become an art. True, these Hebrew versions possess no graces of style, but they rank among the best of their class for fidelity to their originals. Jewish patrons encouraged the translators by material and moral support. Thus, Meshullam of Lunel (twelfth century) was both learned and wealthy, and his eager encouragement of Judah Ibn Tibbon, "the father of Jewish translators," gave a strong impetus to the translating activity of the Jews.

Judah Ibn Tibbon (about 1120-1190) was of Spanish origin, but he emigrated from Granada to Provence during the same persecution that drove Maimonides from his native land. Judah settled in Lunel, and his skill as a physician won him such renown that his medical services were sought by knights and bishops even from across the sea. Judah Ibn Tibbon was a student of science and philosophy. He early qualified himself as a translator by careful attention to philological niceties. Under the inspiration of Meshullam, he spent the years 1161 to 1186 in making a series of translations from Arabic into Hebrew. His translations were difficult and forced in style, but he had no ready-made language at his command. He had to create a new Hebrew. Classical Hebrew was naturally destitute of the technical terms of philosophy, and Ibn Tibbon invented expressions modelled on the Greek and the Arabic. He made Hebrew once more a living language by extending its vocabulary and adapting its idioms to the requirements of medieval culture.

His son Samuel (1160-1230) and his grandson Moses continued the line of faithful but inelegant translators. Judah had turned into Hebrew the works of Bachya, Ibn Gebirol, Jehuda Halevi, Ibn Janach, and Saadiah. Samuel was the translator of Maimonides, and bore a brave part in the defence of his master in the bitter controversies which arose as to the lawfulness and profit of studying philosophy. The translations of the Tibbon family were in the first instance intended for Jewish readers only, but later on the Tibbonite versions were turned into Latin by Buxtorf and others. Another Latin translation of Maimonides existed as early as the thirteenth century.

Of the successors of the Tibbons, Jacob Anatoli (1238) was the first to translate any portion of Averroes into any language. Averroes was an Arab thinker of supreme importance in the Middle Ages, for through his writings Europe was acquainted with Aristotle. Renan asserts that all the early students of Averroes were Jews. Anatoli, a son-in-law of Samuel Ibn Tibbon, was invited by Emperor Frederick II to leave Provence and settle in Naples. To allow Anatoli full leisure for making translations, Frederick granted him an annual income. Anatoli was a friend of the Christian Michael Scot, and the latter made Latin renderings from the former's Hebrew translations. In this way Christian Europe was made familiar with Aristotle as interpreted by Averroes (Ibn Roshd). Much later, the Jew Abraham de Balmes (1523) translated Averroes directly from Arabic into Latin. In the early part of the fourteenth century, Kalonymos, the son of Kalonymos, of Aries (born 1287), translated various works into Latin.

From the thirteenth century onwards, Jews were industrious translators of all the important masterpieces of scientific and philosophical literature. Their zeal included the works of the Greek astronomers and mathematicians, Ptolemy, Euclid, Archimedes, and many others. Alfonso X commissioned several Jews to co-operate with the royal secretaries in making new renderings of older Arabic works on astronomy. Long before this, in 959, the monk Nicholas joined the Jew Chasdai in translating Dioscorides. Most of the Jewish translators were, however, not Spaniards, but Provençals and Italians. It is to them that we owe the Hebrew translations of Galen and Hippocrates, on which Latin versions were based.

The preceding details, mere drops from an ocean of similar facts, show that the Jews were the mediators between Mohammedan and Christian learning in the Middle Ages. According to Lecky, "the Jews were the chief interpreters to Western Europe of Arabian learning." When it is remembered that Arabian learning for a long time included the Greek, it will be seen that Lecky ascribes to Jewish translators a role of the first importance in the history of science. Roger Bacon (1214-1294) had long before said a similar thing: "Michael Scot claimed the merit of numerous translations.

But it is certain that a Jew labored at them more than he did. And so with the rest."

In what precedes, nothing has been said of the *original* contributions made by Jewish authors to scientific literature. Jews were active in original research especially in astronomy, medicine, and mathematics. Many Jewish writers famous as philosophers, Talmudists, or poets, were also men of science. There are numerous Jewish works on the calendar, on astronomical instruments and tables, on mathematics, on medicine, and natural history. Some of their writers share the medieval belief in astrology and magic. But it is noteworthy that Abraham Ibn Ezra doubted the common belief in demons, while Maimonides described astrology as "that error called a science." These subjects, however, are too technical for fuller treatment in the present book. More will be found in the works cited below.

* * * * *

BIBLIOGRAPHY

IBN TIBBON FAMILY.

Graetz.—III, p. 397 [409].

JACOB ANATOLI.

Graetz.—III, p. 566 [584].
Karpeles.—*Sketch of Jewish History* (Jewish Publication Society of America, 1897), pp. 49, 57.

JEWISH TRANSLATORS.

Steinschneider, *Jewish Literature*, p. 62 *seq.*

SCIENCE AND MEDICINE.

Steinschneider.—*Ibid.*, pp. 179 *seq.*, 260 *seq.*
Also, A. Friedenwald.—*Jewish Physicians and the Contributions of the Jews to the Science of Medicine* (*Publications of the Gratz College*, Vol. I).

CHAPTER XV

THE DIFFUSION OF FOLK-TALES

Barlaam and Joshaphat.—The Fables of Bidpai.—Abraham Ibn Chisdai.—Berachya ha-Nakdan.—Joseph Zabara.

The folk-tales of India were communicated to Europe in two ways. First, there was an oral diffusion. In friendly conversation round the family hearth, in the convivial intercourse of the tavern and divan, the wit and wisdom of the East found a home in the West. Having few opportunities of coming into close relations with Christian society, the Jews had only a small share in the oral diffusion of folk-tales. But there was another means of diffusion, namely, by books. By their writings the Jews were able to leave some impress on the popular literature of Europe.

This they did by their translations. Sometimes the Jews translated fables and folk-tales solely for their own use, and in such cases the translations did not leave the Hebrew form into which they were cast. A good example of this was Abraham Ibn Chisdai's "Prince and Nazirite," compiled in the beginning of the thirteenth century. It was a Hebrew version of the legend of Buddha, known as "Barlaam and Joshaphat." In this the story is told of a prince's conversion to the ascetic life. His father had vainly sought to hold him firm to a life of pleasure by isolating him in a beautiful palace, far from the haunts of man, so that he might never know that such things as evil, misery, and death existed. Of course the plan failed, the prince discovered the things hidden from him, and he became converted to the life of self-denial and renunciation associated with the saintly teaching of Buddha. This story is the frame into which a number of charming tales are set, which have found their way into the popular literature of all the world. But in this spread of the Indian stories, the book of Abraham Ibn Chisdai had no part.

Far other it was with the Hebrew translation of the famous Fables of Bidpai, known in Hebrew as *Kalila ve-Dimna*. These fables, like those contained in the "Prince and Nazirite," were Indian, and were in fact birth-stories of Buddha. They were connected by means of a frame, or central plot. A large part of the popular tales of the Middle Ages can be traced to the Fables of Bidpai, and here the Jews exerted important influence. Some authorities even hold that these Fables of Bidpai were brought to Spain directly from India by Jews. This is doubtful, but it is certain that the spread of the Fables was due to Jewish activity. A Jew translated them into Hebrew, and this Hebrew was turned into Latin by the Italian John of Capua, a Jew by birth, in the year 1270. Moreover, the Old Spanish version which was made in 1251 probably was also the work of the Jewish school of translators established in Toledo by Alfonso. The Greek version, which was earlier still, and dates from 1080, was equally the work of a Jew. Thus, as Mr. Joseph Jacobs has shown, this curious collection of fables, which influenced Europe more perhaps than any book except the Bible, started as a Buddhistic work, and passed over to the Mohammedans and Christians chiefly through the mediation of Jews.

Another interesting collection of fables was made by Berachya ha-Nakdan (the Punctuator, or Grammarian). He lived in England in the twelfth century, or according to another opinion he dwelt in France a century later. His collection of 107 "Fox Fables" won wide popularity, for their wit and point combined with their apt use of Biblical phrases to please the medieval taste. The fables in this collection are all old, many of them being Æsop's, but it is very possible that the first knowledge of Æsop gained in England was derived from a Latin translation of Berachya.

Of greater poetical merit was Joseph Zabara's "Book of Delight," written in about the year 1200 in Spain. In this poetical romance a large number of ancient fables and tales are collected, but they are thrown into a frame-work which is partially original. One night he, the author, lay at rest after much toil, when a giant appeared before him, and bade him rise. Joseph hastily obeyed, and by the light of the lamp which the giant carried partook of a fine banquet which his visitor spread for him. Enan, for such was the giant's name, offered to take Joseph to another land, pleasant as a garden, where all men were loving, all men wise. But Joseph refused, and told Enan fable after fable, about leopards, foxes, and lions, all proving that it was best for a man to remain where he was and not travel to foreign places. But Enan coaxes Joseph to go with him, and as they ride on, they tell one another a very long series of excellent tales, and exchange many witty remarks and anecdotes. When at last they reach Enan's city, Joseph discovers that his guide is a demon. In the end, Joseph breaks away from him, and returns home to Barcelona. Now, it is very remarkable that this collection of tales, written in exquisite Hebrew, closely resembles the other collections in which Europe delighted later on. It is hard to believe that Zabara's work had no influence in spreading these tales. At all events, Jews, Christians, and Mohammedans, all read and enjoyed the same stories, all laughed at the same jokes. "It is," says Mr. Jacobs, "one of those touches of nature which make the whole world kin. These folk-tales form a bond, not alone between the ages, but between many races who think they have nothing in common. We have the highest authority that 'out of the mouths of babes and sucklings has the Lord established strength,' and surely of all the influences for good in the world, none is comparable to the lily souls of little children. That Jews, by their diffusion of folk-tales, have furnished so large an amount of material to the childish imagination of the civilized world is, to my mind, no slight thing for Jews to be proud of. It is one of the conceptions that make real to us the idea of the Brotherhood of Man, which, in Jewish minds, is forever associated with the Fatherhood of God."

* * * * *

BIBLIOGRAPHY

J. Jacobs.—*The Diffusion of Folk Tales* (in *Jewish Ideals*, p. 135); *The Fables of Bidpai* (London, 1888) and *Barlaam and Joshaphat* (Introductions).
Steinschneider.—*Jewish Literature*, p. 174.

Berachya Ha-Nakdan,

J. Jacobs.—*Jews of Angevin England*, pp. 165 *seq.*, 278.
A. Neubauer.—*J.Q.R.*, II, p. 520.

Zabara.

I. Abrahams.—*J.Q.R.*, VI, p. 502 (with English translation of
the *Book of Delight*).

CHAPTER XVI

MOSES NACHMANIDES

French and Spanish Talmudists.—The Tossafists, Asher of Speyer, Tam, Isaac of Dompaire, Baruch of Ratisbon, Perez of Corbeil.—Nachmanides' Commentary on the Pentateuch.—Public controversies between Jews and Christians.

Nachmanides was one of the earliest writers to effect a reconciliation between the French and the Spanish schools of Jewish literature. On the one side, his Spanish birth and training made him a friend of the widest culture; on the other, he was possessed of the French devotion to the Talmud. Moses, the son of Nachman (Nachmanides, Ramban, 1195-1270), Spaniard though he was, says, "The French Rabbis have won most Jews to their view. They are our masters in Talmud, and to them we must go for instruction." From the eleventh to the fourteenth century, a French school of Talmudists occupied themselves with the elucidation of the Talmud, and from the "Additions" (*Tossafoth*) which they compiled they are known as Tossafists. The Tossafists were animated with an altogether different spirit from that of the Spanish writers on the Talmud. But though their method is very involved and over-ingenious, they display so much mastery of the Talmud, such excellent discrimination, and so keen a critical insight, that they well earned the fame they have enjoyed. The earliest Tossafists were the family and pupils of Rashi, but the method spread from Northern France to Provence, and thence to Spain. The most famous Tossafists were Isaac, the son of Asher of Speyer (end of the eleventh century); Tam of Rameru (Rashi's grandson);

Isaac the Elder of Dompaire (Tam's nephew); Baruch of Ratisbon; and Perez of Corbeil.

Nachmanides' admiration for the French method—a method by no means restricted to the Tossafists—did not blind him to its defects. "They try to force an elephant through the eye of a needle," he sarcastically said of some of the French casuists. Nachmanides thus possessed some of the independence characteristic of the Spanish Jews. He also shared the poetic spirit of Spain, and his hymn for the Day of Atonement is one of the finest products of the new-Hebrew muse. The last stanzas run thus:

> Thine is the love, O God, and thine the grace,
> That holds the sinner in its mild embrace;
> Thine the forgiveness, bridging o'er the space
>> 'Twixt man's works and the task set by the King.

> Unheeding all my sins, I cling to thee!
> I know that mercy shall thy footstool be:
> Before I call, O do thou answer me,
>> For nothing dare I claim of thee, my King!

> O thou, who makest guilt to disappear,
> My help, my hope, my rock, I will not fear;
> Though thou the body hold in dungeon drear,
>> The soul has found the palace of the King!

Everything that Nachmanides wrote is warm with tender love. He was an enthusiast in many directions. His heart went out to the French Talmudists, yet he cherished so genuine an affection for Maimonides that he defended him with spirit against his detractors. Gentle by nature, he broke forth into fiery indignation against the French critics of Maimonides. At the same time his tender soul was attracted by the emotionalism of the Kabbala, or mystical view of life, a view equally opposed to the views of Maimonides and of the French school. He tried to act the part of reconciler, but his intellect, strong as it was, was too much at the mercy of his emotions for him to win a commanding place in the controversies of his time.

For a moment we may turn aside from his books to the incidents of his life. Like Maimonides, he was a physician by profession and a Rabbi by way of leisure. The most momentous incident in his career in Barcelona was his involuntary participation in a public dispute with a convert from the Synagogue. Pablo Christiani burned with the desire to convert the Jews *en masse* to Christianity, and in 1263 he induced King Jayme I of Aragon to summon Nachmanides to a controversy on the truth of Christianity. Nachmanides complied with the royal command most reluctantly. He felt that the process of rousing theological animosity by a public discussion could only end in a religious persecution. However, he had no alternative but to assent. He stipulated for complete freedom of speech. This was granted, but when Nachmanides published his version of the discussion, the Dominicans were incensed. True, the special commission appointed to examine the charge of blasphemy brought against Nachmanides reported that he had merely availed himself of the right of free speech which had been guaranteed to him. He was nevertheless sentenced to exile, and his pamphlet was burnt. Nachmanides was seventy years of age at the time. He settled in Palestine, where he died in about 1270, amid a band of devoted friends and disciples, who did not, however, reconcile him to the separation from his Spanish home. "I left my family," he wrote, "I forsook my house. There, with my sons and daughters, the sweet, dear children whom I brought up on my knees, I left also my soul My heart and my eyes will dwell with them forever."

The Halachic, or Talmudical, works of Nachmanides have already been mentioned. His homiletical, or exegetical, writings are of more literary importance. In "The Sacred Letter" he contended that man's earthly nature is divine no less than his soul, and he vindicates the "flesh" from the attacks made on human character by certain forms of Christianity. The body, according to Nachmanides, is, with all its functions, the work of God, and therefore perfect. "It is only sin and neglect that disfigure God's creatures." In another of his books, "The Law of Man," Nachmanides writes of suffering and death. He offers an antidote to pessimism, for he boldly asserts that pain and suffering in themselves are "a service of God, leading man to ponder on his end and reflect about his destiny." Nachmanides believed in the bodily resurrection, but held that the soul was in a special sense a direct emanation from God. He was not a philosopher strictly so-called; he was a mystic more than a thinker, one to whom God was an intuition, not a concept of reason.

The greatest work of Nachmanides was his "Commentary on the Pentateuch." He reveals his whole character in it. In composing his work he had, he tells us, three motives, an intellectual, a theological, and an emotional motive. First, he would "satisfy the minds of students, and draw their heart out by a critical examination of the text." His exposition is, indeed, based on true philology and on deep and original study of the Bible. His style is peculiarly attractive, and had he been content to offer a plain commentary, his work would have ranked among the best. But he had other desires besides giving a simple explanation of the text. He had, secondly, a theological motive, to justify God and discover in the words of Scripture a hidden meaning. In the Biblical narratives, Nachmanides sees *types* of the history of man. Thus, the account of the six days of creation is turned into a prophecy of the events which would occur during the next six thousand years, and the seventh day is a type of the millennium. So, too, Nachmanides finds symbolical senses in Scriptural texts, "for, in the Torah, are hidden every wonder and every mystery, and in her treasures is sealed every beauty of wisdom." Finally, Nachmanides wrote, not only for educational and theological ends, but also for edification. His third purpose was "to bring peace to the minds of students (laboring under persecution and trouble), when they read the portion of the Pentateuch on Sabbaths and festivals, and to attract their hearts by simple explanations and sweet words." His own enthusiastic and loving temperament speaks in this part of his commentary. It is true, as Graetz says, that Nachmanides exercised more influence on his contemporaries and on succeeding ages by his personality than by his writings. But it must be added that the writings of Nachmanides are his personality.

* * * * *

BIBLIOGRAPHY

Manides.

    I.H. Weiss, *Study of the Talmud in the Thirteenth Century*, *J.Q.R.*, I, p. 289.

    S. Schechter.—*Studies in Judaism*, p. 99 [120].

Graetz.—III, 17; also III, p. 598 [617].

JACOB TAM.

Graetz.—III, p. 375 [385].

TOSSAFISTS.

Graetz.—III, p. 344 [351], 403 [415].

CHAPTER XVII

THE ZOHAR AND LATER MYSTICISM

Kabbala.—The Bahir.—Abulafia.—Moses of Leon.—The Zohar.—Isaac Lurya.—Isaiah Hurwitz.—Christian Kabbalists.—The Chassidim.

Mysticism is the name given to the belief in direct, intuitive communion with God. All true religion has mystical elements, for all true religion holds that man can commune with God, soul with soul. In the Psalms, God is the Rock of the heart, the Portion of the cup, the Shepherd and Light, the Fountain of Life, an exceeding Joy. All this is, in a sense, *mystical* language. But mysticism has many dangers. It is apt to confuse vague emotionalism and even hysteria with communion with God. A further defect of mysticism is that, in its medieval forms, it tended to the multiplication of intermediate beings, or angels, which it created to supply the means for that communion with God which, in theory, the mystics asserted was direct. Finally, from being a deep-seated, emotional aspect of religion, mysticism degenerated into intellectual sport, a play with words and a juggling with symbols.

Jewish mysticism passed through all these stages. Kabbala—as mysticism was called—really means "Tradition," and the name proves that the theory had its roots far back in the past. It has just been said that there is mysticism in the Psalms. So there is in the idea of inspiration, the prophet's receiving a message direct from God with whom he spoke face to face. After the prophetic age, Jewish mysticism displayed itself in intense personal religiousness, as well as in love for Apocalyptic, or dream, literature, in which the sleeper could, like Daniel, feel himself lapped to rest in the bosom of God.

All the earlier literary forms of mysticism, or theosophy, made comparatively little impression on Jewish writers. But at the beginning of the thirteenth century a great development took place in the "secret" science of the Kabbala. The very period which produced the rationalism of Maimonides gave birth to the emotionalism of the Kabbala. The Kabbala was at first a protest against too much intellectualism and rigidity in religion. It reclaimed religion for the heart. A number of writers more or less dallied with the subject, and then the Kabbala took a bolder flight. Ezra, or Azriel, a teacher of Nachmanides, compiled a book called "Brilliancy" (*Bahir*) in the year 1240. It was at once regarded as a very ancient book. As will be seen, the same pretence of antiquity was made with regard to another famous Kabbalistic work of a later generation. Under Todros Abulafia (1234-1304) and Abraham Abulafia (1240-1291), the mystical movement took a practical shape, and the Jewish masses were much excited by stories of miracles performed and of the appearance of a new Messiah.

At this moment Moses of Leon (born in Leon in about 1250, died in Arevalo in 1305) wrote the most famous Kabbalistic book of the Middle Ages. This was named, in imitation of the Bahir, "Splendor" (*Zohar*), and its brilliant success matched its title. Not only did this extraordinary book raise the Kabbala to the zenith of its influence, but it gave it a firm and, as it has proved, unassailable basis. Like the Bahir, the Zohar was not offered to the public on its own merits, but was announced as the work of Simon, the son of Yochai, who lived in the second century. The Zohar, it was pretended, had been concealed in a cavern in Galilee for more than a thousand years, and had now been suddenly discovered. The Zohar is, indeed, a work of genius, its spiritual beauty, its fancy, its daring imagery, its depth of devotion, ranking it among the great books of the world. Its literary style, however, is less meritorious; it is difficult and involved. As Chatterton clothed his ideas in a pseudo-archaic English, so Moses of Leon used an Aramaic idiom, which he handled clumsily and not as one to the manner born. It would not be so important to insist on the fact that the Zohar was a literary forgery, that it pretended to an antiquity it did not own, were it not that many Jews and Christians still write as though they believe that the book is as old as it was asserted to be. The defects of the Zohar are in keeping with this imposture. Absurd allegories are read into the Bible; the words of Scripture are counters in a game of distortion and combination; God himself is obscured amid a maze of mystic beings, childishly conceived and childishly named. Philosophically, the Zohar has no originality. Its doctrines of the Transmigration of the Soul, of the Creation as God's self-revelation in the world, of the Emanation from the divine essence of semi-human, semi-divine powers, were only commonplaces of medieval theology. Its great original idea was that the revealed Word of God, the Torah, was designed for no other purpose than to effect a union between the soul of man and the soul of God.

Reinforced by this curious jumble of excellence and nonsense, the Kabbala became one of the strongest literary bonds between Jews and Christians. It is hardly to be wondered at, for the Zohar contains some ideas which are more Christian than Jewish. Christians, like Pico di Mirandola (1463-1494), under the influence of the Jewish Kabbalist Jochanan Aleman, and Johann Reuchlin (1455-1522), sharer of Pico's spirit and precursor of the improved study of the Scriptures in Europe, made the Zohar the basis of their defence of Jewish literature against the attempts of various ecclesiastical bodies to crush and destroy it.

The Kabbala did not, however, retain a high place in the realm of literature. It greatly influenced Jewish religious ceremonies, it produced saintly souls, and from such centres as Safed and Salonica sent forth men like Solomon Molcho and Sabbatai Zevi, who maintained that they were Messiahs, and could perform miracles on the strength of Kabbalistic powers. But from the literary standpoint the Kabbala was a barren inspiration. The later works of Kabbalists are a rehash of the older works. The Zohar was the bible of the Kabbalists, and the later works of the school were commentaries on this bible. The Zohar had absorbed all the earlier Kabbalistic literature, such as the "Book of Creation" (*Sefer Yetsirah*), the Book Raziel, the Alphabet of Rabbi Akiba, and it was the final literary expression of the Kabbala.

It is, therefore, unnecessary to do more than name one or two of the more noted Kabbalists of post-Zoharistic ages. Isaac Lurya (1534-1572) was a saint, so devoid of self-conceit that he published nothing, though he flourished at the very time when the printing-press was throwing copies of the Zohar broadcast. We owe our knowledge of Lurya's Kabbalistic ideas to the prolific writings of his disciple Chayim Vital Calabrese, who died in Damascus in 1620. Other famous Kabbalists were Isaiah Hurwitz (about 1570-1630), author of a much admired ethical work, "The Two Tables of the Covenant" (*Sheloh*, as it is familiarly called from the initials of its Hebrew title); Nehemiah Chayun (about 1650-1730); and the Hebrew dramatist Moses Chayim Luzzatto (1707-1747).

A more recent Kabbalistic movement, led by the founder of the new saints, or Chassidim, Israel Baalshem (about 1700-1772), was even less literary than the one just described. But the Kabbalists, medieval and modern, were meritorious writers in one field of literature. The Kabbalists and the Chassidim were the authors of some of the most exquisite prayers and meditations which the soul of the Jew has poured forth since the Psalms were completed. This redeems the later Kabbalistic literature from the altogether unfavorable verdict which would otherwise have to be passed on it.

* * * * *

BIBLIOGRAPHY

KABBALA.

> Graetz.—III, p. 547 [565]

S DE LEON.

> Graetz.—IV, 1.

ZOHAR.

> A. Neubauer.—*Bahir and Zohar, J.Q.R.*, IV, p. 357.
> Steinschneider.—*Jewish Literature*, p. 104.

ISAAC LURYA.

> Graetz.—IV, p. 618 [657].

Sabbatai Zevi.

>Graetz.—V, p. 118 [125].

Chassidim.

>Graetz.—V, 9.
>Schechter.—*Studies in Judaism*, p. 1.

CHAPTER XVIII

ITALIAN JEWISH POETRY

Immanuel and Dante.—The Machberoth.—Judah Romano.—
Kalonymos.—The Eben Bochan.—Moses Rieti.—Messer Leon.

The course of Jewish literature in Italy ran along the same
lines as in Spain. The Italian group of authors was less brilliant,
but the difference was one of degree, not of kind. The Italian
aristocracy, like the Moorish caliphs and viziers, patronized learning,
and encouraged the Jews in their literary ambitions.

Yet the fact that the inspiration in Spain came from Islam
and in Italy from Christianity produced some consequences. In
Spain the Jews followed Arab models of style. In Italy the influence
of classical models was felt at the time of the Renaissance. Most
noteworthy of all was the indebtedness of the Hebrew poets of
Italy to Dante.

It is not improbable that Dante was a personal friend of
the most noted of these Jewish poets, Immanuel, the son of
Solomon of Rome. Like the other Jews of Rome, Immanuel stood
in the most friendly relations with Christians, for nowhere was
medieval intolerance less felt than in the very seat of the Pope,
the head of the Church. Thus, on the one hand Immanuel was a
leading member of the synagogue, and, on the other, he carried
on a literary correspondence with learned Christians, with poets,
and men of science. He was himself a physician, and his poems
breathe a scientific spirit. As happened earlier in Spain, the circle
of Immanuel regarded verse-making as part of the culture of a
scholar. Witty verses, in the form of riddles and epigrams, were

exchanged at the meetings of the circle. With these poets, among whom Kalonymos was included, the penning of verses was a fashion. On the other hand, music was not so much cultivated by the Italian Hebrews as by the Spanish. Hence, both Immanuel and Kalonymos lack the lightness and melody of the best writers of Hebrew verse in Spain. The Italians atoned for this loss by their subject-matter. They are joyous poets, full of the gladness of life. They are secular, not religious poets; the best of the Spanish-Hebrew poetry was devotional, and the best of the Italian so secular that it was condemned by pietists as too frivolous and too much "disfigured by ill-timed levity."

Immanuel was born in Rome in about 1270. He rarely mentions his father, but often names his mother Justa as a woman of pious and noble character. As a youth, he had a strong fancy for scientific study, and was nourished on the "Guide" of Maimonides, on the works of the Greeks and Arabs, and on the writings of the Christian school-men, which he read in Hebrew translations. Besides philosophy, mathematics, astronomy, and medicine, Immanuel studied the Bible and the Talmud, and became an accomplished scholar. He was not born a poet, but he read deeply the poetical literature of Jews and Christians, and took lessons in rhyme-making. He was wealthy, and his house was a rendezvous of wits and scientists. His own position in the Jewish community was remarkable. It has already been said that he took an active part in the management of communal affairs, but he did more than this. He preached in the synagogue on the Day of Atonement, and delivered eulogistic orations over the remains of departed worthies. Towards the end of his life he suffered losses both in fortune and in friends, but he finally found a new home in Fermo, where he was cordially welcomed in 1328. The date of his death is uncertain, but he died in about 1330.

His works were versatile rather than profound. He wrote grammatical treatises and commentaries, which display learning more than originality. But his poetical writings are of great interest in the history of Jewish literature. He lived in the dawn-flush of the Renaissance in Italy. The Italian language was just evolving itself, under the genius of Dante, from a mere jumble of dialects into a literary language. Dante did for Italy what Chaucer was soon after to do for England. On the one side influenced by the Renaissance and the birth of the new Italian language, on the other by the Jewish revival of letters in Spain and Provence, the Italian Jews alone combined the Jewish spirit with the spirit of the classical Renaissance. Immanuel was the incarnation of this complex soul.

This may be seen from the form of Immanuel's *Machberoth*, or "Collection." The latter portion of it, named separately "Hell and Eden," was imitated from the Christian Dante; the poem as a whole was planned on Charizi's *Tachkemoni*, a Hebrew development of the Arabic Divan. The poet is not the hero of his own song, but like the Arabic poets of the divan, conceives a personage who fills the centre of the canvas—a personage really identical with the author, yet in a sense other than he. Much quaintness of effect is produced by this double part played by the poet, who, as it were, satirizes his own doings. In Immanuel's *Machberoth* there is much variety of romantic incident. But it is in satire that he reaches his highest level. Love and wine are the frequent burdens of his song, as they are in the Provençal and Italian poetry of his day. Immanuel was something of a Voltaire in his jocose treatment of sacred things, and pietists like Joseph Karo inhibited the study of the *Machberoth*. Others, too, described his songs as sensuous and his satires as blasphemous. But the devout and earnest piety of some of Immanuel's prayers,—some of them to be found in the *Machberoth* themselves—proves that Immanuel's licentiousness and levity were due, not to lack of reverence, but to the attempt to reconcile the ideals of Italian society of the period of the Renaissance with the ideals of Judaism.

Immanuel owed his rhymed prose to Charizi, but again he shows his devotion to two masters by writing Hebrew sonnets. The sonnet was new then to Italian verse, and Immanuel's Hebrew specimens thus belong to the earliest sonnets written in any literature. It is, indeed, impossible to convey a just sense of the variety of subject and form in the *Machberoth*. "Serious and frivolous topics trip each other by the heels; all metrical forms, prayers, elegies, passages in unmetrical rhymes, all are mingled together." The last chapter is, however, of a different character, and it has often been printed as a separate work. It is the "Hell and Eden" to which allusion has already been made.

The link between Immanuel and his Provençal contemporary Kalonymos was supplied by Judah Romano, the Jewish school-man.

All three were in the service of the king of Naples. Kalonymos was the equal of Romano as a philosopher and not much below Immanuel as a satirist. He was a more fertile poet than Immanuel, for, while Immanuel remained the sole representative of his manner, Kalonymos gave birth to a whole school of imitators. Kalonymos wrote many translations, of Galen, Averroes, Aristotle, al-Farabi, Ptolemy, and Archimedes. But it was his keen wit more than his learning that made him popular in Rome, and impelled the Jews of that city, headed by Immanuel, to persuade Kalonymos to settle permanently in Italy. Kalonymos' two satirical poems were called "The Touchstone" (*Eben Bochan*) and "The Purim Tractate." These satirize the customs and social habits of the Jews of his day in a bright and powerful style. In his Purim Tractate, Kalonymos parodies the style, logic, and phraseology of the Talmud, and his work was the forerunner of a host of similar parodies.

There were many Italian writers of *Piyutim*, i.e. Synagogue hymns, but these were mediocre in merit. The elegies written in lament for the burning of the Law and the martyrdoms endured in various parts of Italy were the only meritorious devotional poems composed in Hebrew in that country. Italy remained famous in Hebrew poetry for secular, not for religious compositions. In the fifteenth century Moses Rieti (born 1389, died later than 1452) imitated Dante once more in his "Lesser Sanctuary" (*Mikdash Meät*). Here again may be noticed a feature peculiar to Italian Hebrew poetry. Rieti uses regular stanzas, Italian forms of verse, in this matter following the example of Immanuel. Messer Leon, a physician of Mantua, wrote a treatise on Biblical rhetoric (1480). Again, the only important writer of dramas in Hebrew was, as we shall see, an Italian Jew, who copied Italian models. Though, therefore, the Hebrew poetry of Italy scarcely reaches the front rank, it is historically of first-rate importance. It represents the only effects of the Renaissance on Jewish literature. In other countries, the condition of the Jews was such that they were shut off from external influences. Their literature suffered as their lives did from imprisonment within the Ghettos, which were erected both by the Jews themselves and by the governments of Europe.

* * * * *

BIBLIOGRAPHY

S. Morals.—*Italian Jewish Literature* (*Publications of the Gratz College*, Vol. 1).

IMMANUEL AND KALONYMOS.

Graetz.—IV, p. 61 [66].

J. Chotzner.—*Immanuel di Romi*, *J.Q.*R., IV, p. 64.

G. Sacerdote.—*Emanuele da Roma's Ninth Mehabbereth*, *J.Q.*R., VII, p. 711.

JUDAH (LEONE) ROMANO.

Graetz.—IV, p. 68 [73].

MOSES RIETI.

Graetz.—IV, p. 230 [249].

MESSER LEON.

Graetz.—IV, p. 289 [311].

CHAPTER XIX

ETHICAL LITERATURE

Bachya Ibn Pekuda.—Choboth ha-Lebaboth.—Sefer ha-Chassidim.—Rokeach.—Yedaiah Bedaressi's Bechinath Olam.—Isaac Aboab's Menorath ha-Maor.—Ibn Chabib's "Eye of Jacob."—Zevaoth, or Ethical Wills.—Joseph Ibn Caspi.—Solomon Alami.

A large proportion of all Hebrew books is ethical. Many of the works already treated here fall under this category. The Talmudical, exegetical, and philosophical writings of Jews were also ethical treatises. In this chapter, however, attention will be restricted to a few books which are in a special sense ethical.

Collections of moral proverbs, such as the "Choice of Pearls," attributed to Ibn Gebirol, and the "Maxims of the Philosophers" by Charizi, were great favorites in the Middle Ages. They had a distinct charm, but they were not original. They were either compilations from older books or direct translations from the Arabic. It was far otherwise with the ethical work entitled "Heart Duties" (*Choboth ha-Lebaboth*), by Bachya Ibn Pekuda (about 1050-1100). This was as original as it was forcible. Bachya founded his ethical system on the Talmud and on the philosophical notions current in his day, but he evolved out of these elements an original view of life. The inner duties dictated by conscience were set above all conventional morality. Bachya probed the very heart of religion. His soul was filled with God, and this communion, despite the ascetic feelings to which it gave rise, was to Bachya an exceeding joy. His book thrills the reader with the author's own chastened enthusiasm. The "Heart Duties" of Bachya is the most inspired book written by a Jew in the Middle Ages.

In part worthy of a place by the side of Bachya's treatise is an ethical book written in the Rhinelands during the thirteenth century. "The Book of the Pious" (*Sefer ha-Chassidim*) is mystical, and in course of time superstitious elements were interpolated. Wrongly attributed to a single writer, Judah Chassid, the "Book of the Pious" was really the combined product of the Jewish spirit in the thirteenth century. It is a conglomerate of the sublime and the trivial, the purely ethical with the ceremonial. With this popular and remarkable book may be associated other conglomerates of the ritual, the ethical, and the mystical, as the *Rokeach* by Eleazar of Worms.

A simpler but equally popular work was Yedaiah Bedaressi's "Examination of the World" (*Bechinath Olam*), written in about the year 1310. Its style is florid but poetical, and the many quaint turns which it gives to quotations from the Bible remind the reader of Ibn Gebirol. Its earnest appeal to man to aim at the higher life, its easily intelligible and commonplace morals, endeared it to the "general reader" of the Middle Ages. Few books have been more often printed, few more often translated.

Another favorite class of ethical books consisted of compilations made direct from the Talmud and the Midrash. The oldest and most prized of these was Isaac Aboab's "Lamp of Light" (*Menorath ha-Maor*). It was an admirably written book, clearly arranged, and full to the brim of ethical gems. Aboab's work was written between 1310 and 1320. It is arranged according to subjects, differing in this respect from another very popular compilation, Jacob Ibn Chabib's "Eye of Jacob" (*En Yaakob*), which was completed in the sixteenth century. In this, the Hagadic passages of the Talmud are extracted without arrangement, the order of the Talmud itself being retained. The "Eye of Jacob" was an extremely popular work.

Of the purely devotional literature of Judaism, it is impossible to speak here. One other ethical book must be here noticed, for it has attained wide and deserved popularity. This is the "Path of the Upright" (*Messilath Yesharim*) by Moses Chayim Luzzatto, of whom more will be said in a later chapter. But a little more space must be here devoted to a species of ethical tract which was peculiar to Jewish moralists. These tracts were what are known as Ethical Wills.

These Ethical Wills (*Zevaoth*) contained the express directions of fathers to their children or of aged teachers to their disciples. They were for the most part written calmly in old age, but not immediately before the writers' death. Some of them were very carefully composed, and amount to formal ethical treatises. But in the main they are charmingly natural and unaffected. They were intended for the absolutely private use of children and relatives, or of some beloved pupil who held the dearest place in his master's regard. They were not designed for publication, and thus, as the writer had no reason to expect that his words would pass beyond a limited circle, the Ethical Will is a clear revelation of his innermost feelings and ideals. Intellectually some of these Ethical Wills are poor; morally, however, the general level is very high.

Addresses of parents to their children occur in the Bible, the Apocrypha, and the Rabbinical literature. But the earliest extant Ethical Will written as an independent document is that of Eleazar, the son of Isaac of Worms (about 1050), who must not be confused with the author of the *Rokeach*. The eleventh and twelfth centuries supply few examples of the Ethical Will, but from the thirteenth century onwards there is a plentiful array of them. "Think not of evil," says Eleazar of Worms, "for evil thinking leads to evil doing . . . Purify thy body, the dwelling-place of thy soul . . . Give of all thy food a portion to God. Let God's portion be the best, and give it to the poor." The will of the translator Judah Ibn Tibbon (about 1190) contains at least one passage worthy of Ruskin: "Avoid bad society, make thy books thy companions, let thy book-cases and shelves be thy gardens and pleasure-grounds. Pluck the fruit that grows therein, gather the roses, the spices, and the myrrh. If thy soul be satiate and weary, change from garden to garden, from furrow to furrow, from sight to sight. Then will thy desire renew itself, and thy soul be satisfied with delight." The will of Nachmanides is an unaffected eulogy of humility. Asher, the son of Yechiel (fourteenth century), called his will "Ways of Life," and it includes 132 maxims, which are often printed in the prayer-book. "Do not obey the Law for reward, nor avoid sin from fear of punishment, but serve God from love. Sleep not over-much, but rise with the birds. Be not over-hasty to reply to offensive remarks; raise not thy hand against another, even if he curse thy father or mother in thy presence."

Some of these wills, like that of the son of the last mentioned, are written in rhymed prose; some are controversial. Joseph Ibn Caspi writes in 1322: "How can I know God, and that he is one, unless I know what knowing means, and what constitutes unity? Why should these things be left to non-Jewish philosophers? Why should Aristotle retain sole possession of the treasures that he stole from Solomon?" The belief that Aristotle had visited Jerusalem with Alexander the Great, and there obtained possession of Solomon's wisdom, was one of the most curious myths of the Middle Ages. The will of Eleazar the Levite of Mainz (1357) is a simple document, without literary merit, but containing a clear exposition of duty. "Judge every man charitably, and use your best efforts to find a kindly explanation of conduct, however suspicious . . . Give in charity an exact tithe of your property. Never turn a poor man away empty-handed. Talk no more than is necessary, and thus avoid slander. Be not as dumb cattle that utter no word of gratitude, but thank God for his bounties at the time at which they occur, and in your prayers let the memory of these personal favors warm your hearts, and prompt you to special fervor during the utterance of the communal thanks for communal well-being. When words of thanks occur in the liturgy, pause and silently reflect on the goodness of God to you that day."

In striking contrast to the simplicity of the foregoing is the elaborate "Letter of Advice" by Solomon Alami (beginning of the fifteenth century). It is composed in beautiful rhymed prose, and is an important historical record. For the author shared the sufferings of the Jews of the Iberian peninsula in 1391, and this gives pathetic point to his counsel: "Flee without hesitation when exile is the only means of securing religious freedom; have no regard to your worldly career or your property, but go at once."

It is needless to indicate fully the nature of the Ethical Wills of the sixteenth and subsequent centuries. They are closely similar to the foregoing, but they tend to become more learned and less simple. Yet, though as literature they are often quite insignificant, as ethics they rarely sink below mediocrity.

* * * * *

BIBLIOGRAPHY

ETHICAL LITERATURE.

Steinschneider.—*Jewish Literature*, pp. 100, 232.

B.H. Ascher.—*Choice of Pearls* (with English translation, London, 1859).

D. Rosin.—*Ethics of Solomon Ibn Gebirol*, *J.Q.R.*, III, p. 159.

BACHYA.

Graetz, III, p. 271.

YEDAYA BEDARESSI.

Graetz.—IV, p. 42 [45].

J. Chotzner.—*J.Q.R.*, VIII, p. 414.

T. Goodman.—English translation of *Bechinath Olam* (London, 1830).

ETHICAL WILLS.

Edelmann.—*The Path of Good Men* (London, 1852).

I. Abrahams, *J.Q.R.*, III, p. 436.

CHAPTER XX

TRAVELLERS' TALES

Eldad the Danite.—Benjamin of Tudela.—Petachiah of Ratisbon.—Esthori Parchi.—Abraham Farissol.—David Reubeni and Molcho.—Antonio de Montesinos and Manasseh ben Israel.—Tobiah Cohen.—Wessely.

The voluntary and enforced travels of the Jews produced, from the earliest period after the destruction of the Temple, an extensive, if fragmentary, geographical literature. In the Talmud and later religious books, in the Letters of the Gaonim, in the correspondence of Jewish ambassadors, in the autobiographical narratives interspersed in the works of all Jewish scholars of the Middle Ages, in the *Aruch*, or Talmudical Lexicon, of Nathan of Rome, in the satirical romances of the poetical globe-trotters, Zabara and Charizi, and, finally, in the Bible commentaries written by Jews, many geographical notes are to be found. But the composition of complete works dedicated to travel and exploration dates only from the twelfth century.

Before that time, however, interest in the whereabouts of the Lost Ten Tribes gave rise to a book which has been well called the Arabian Nights of the Jews. The "Diary of Eldad the Danite," written in about the year 880, was a popular romance, to which additions and alterations were made at various periods. This diary tells of mighty Israelite empires, especially of the tribe of Moses, the peoples of which were all virtuous, all happy, and long-lived.

"A river flows round their land for a distance of four days' journey on every side. They dwell in beautiful houses provided with handsome towers, which they have built themselves. There is nothing unclean among them, neither in the case of birds, venison, nor domesticated animals; there are no wild beasts, no flies, no foxes, no vermin, no serpents, no dogs, and, in general, nothing that does harm; they have only sheep and cattle, which bear twice a year. They sow and reap, they have all kinds of gardens with all kinds of fruits and cereals, beans, melons, gourds, onions, garlic, wheat, and barley, and the seed grows a hundredfold. They have faith; they know the Law, the Mishnah, the Talmud, and the Hagadah . . . No child, be it son or daughter, dies during the life-time of its parents, but they reach a third and fourth generation. They do all the field-work themselves, having no male nor female servants. They do not close their houses at night, for there is no thief or evil-doer among them. They have plenty of gold and silver; they sow flax, and cultivate the crimson-worm, and make beautiful garments . . . The river Sambatyon is two hundred yards broad, about as far as a bow-shot. It is full of sand and stones, but without water; the stones make a great noise, like the waves of the sea and a stormy wind, so that in the night the noise is heard at a distance of half a day's journey. There are fish in it, and all kinds of clean birds fly round it. And this river of stone and sand rolls during the six working-days, and rests on the Sabbath day. As soon as the Sabbath begins, fire surrounds the river, and the flames remain till the next evening, when the Sabbath ends. Thus no human being can reach the river for a distance of half a mile on either side; the fire consumes all that grows there."

With wild rapture the Jews of the ninth century heard of these prosperous and powerful kingdoms. Hopes of a restoration to former dignity encouraged them to believe in the mythical narrative of Eldad. It is doubtful whether he was a *bona fide* traveller. At all events, his book includes much that became the legendary property of all peoples in the Middle Ages, such as the fable of the mighty Christian Emperor of India, Prester John.

Some further account of this semi-mythical monarch is contained in the first real Jewish traveller's book, the "Itinerary" of Benjamin of Tudela. This Benjamin was a merchant, who, in the year 1160, started on a long journey, which was prompted partly by commercial, partly by scientific motives. He visited a large part of Europe and Asia, went to Jerusalem and Bagdad, and gives in his "Itinerary" some remarkable geographical facts and some equally remarkable fables. He tells, for instance, the story of the pretended Messiah, David Alroy, whom Disraeli made the hero of one of his romances. Benjamin of Tudela's "Itinerary" was a real contribution to geography.

Soon after Benjamin, another Jew, Petachiah of Ratisbon, set out on a similar but less extended tour, which occupied him during the years 1179 and 1180. His "Travels" are less informing than those of his immediate predecessor, but his descriptions of the real or reputed sepulchres of ancient worthies and his account of the Jewish College in Bagdad are full of romantic interest, which was not lessened for medieval readers because much of Petachiah's narrative was legendary.

A far more important work was written by the first Jewish explorer of Palestine, Esthori Parchi, a contemporary of Mandeville. His family originated in Florenza, in Andalusia, and the family name Parchi (the Flower) was derived from this circumstance. Esthori was himself born in Provence, and was a student of science as well as of the Talmud. When he, together with the rest of the Jews of France, was exiled in 1306, he wandered to Spain and Egypt until the attraction of the Holy Land proved irresistible. His manner was careful, and his love of accuracy unusual for his day. Hence, he was not content to collect all ancient and contemporary references to the sites of Palestine. For seven years he devoted himself to a personal exploration of the country, two years being passed in Galilee. In 1322 he completed his work, which he called *Kaphtor va-Pherach* (Bunch and Flower) in allusion to his own name.

Access to the Holy Land became easier for Jews in the fourteenth century. Before that time the city of Jerusalem had for a considerable period been barred to Jewish pilgrims. By the laws of Constantine and of Omar no Jew might enter within the precincts of his ancient capital. Even in the centuries subsequent to Omar, such pilgrimages were fraught with danger, but the poems of Jehuda Halevi, the tolerance of Islam, and the reputation of Northern Syria as a centre of the Kabbala, combined to draw many Jews to Palestine. Many letters and narratives were the results. One characteristic specimen must suffice. In 1488 Obadiah of Bertinoro, author of the most popular commentary on the Mishnah, removed from Italy to Jerusalem, where he was appointed Rabbi. In a letter to his father he gives an intensely moving account of his voyage and of the state of Hebron and Zion. The narrative is full of personal detail, and is marked throughout by deep love for his father, which struggles for the mastery with his love for the Holy City.

A more ambitious work was the "Itinera Mundi" of Abraham Farissol, written in the autumn of 1524. This treatise was based upon original researches as well as on the works of Christian and Arabian geographers. He incidentally says a good deal about the condition of the Jews in various parts of the world. Indeed, almost all the geographical writings of Jews are social histories of their brethren in faith. Somewhat later, David Reubeni published some strange stories as to the Jews. He went to Rome, where he made a considerable sensation, and was received by Pope Clement VII (1523-1534). Dwarfish in stature and dark in complexion, David Reubeni was wasted by continual fasting, but his manner, though harsh and forbidding, was intrepid and awe-inspiring. His outrageous falsehoods for a time found ready acceptance with Jews and Christians alike, and his fervid Messianism won over to his cause many Marranos—Jews who had been forced by the Inquisition in Spain to assume the external garb of Christianity. His chief claim on the memory of posterity was his connection with the dramatic career of Solomon Molcho (1501-1532), a youth noble in mind and body, who at Reubeni's instigation personated the Messiah, and in early manhood died a martyr's death amid the flames of the Inquisition at Mantua.

The geographical literature of the Jews did not lose its association with Messianic hopes. Antonio de Montesinos, in 1642, imagined that he had discovered in South America the descendants of the Ten Tribes. He had been led abroad by business considerations and love of travel, and in Brazil came across a mestizo Indian, from whose statements he conceived the firm belief that the Ten Tribes resided and thrived in Brazil. Two years later he visited Amsterdam, and, his imagination aflame with the hopes which had not been stifled by several years' endurance of the prisons and tortures of the Inquisition, persuaded Manasseh ben Israel to accept his statements. On his death-bed in Brazil, Montesinos reiterated his assertions, and Manasseh ben Israel not only founded thereon his noted book, "The Hope of Israel," but under the inspiration of similar ideas felt impelled to visit London, and win from Cromwell the right of the Jews to resettle in England.

Jewish geographical literature grew apace in the eighteenth century. A famous book, the "Work of Tobiah," was written at the beginning of this period by Tobiah Cohen, who was born at Metz in 1652, and died in Jerusalem in 1729. It is a medley of science and fiction, an encyclopedia dealing with all branches of knowledge. He had studied at the Universities of Frankfort and Padua, had enjoyed the patronage of the Elector of Brandenburg, and his medical knowledge won him many distinguished patients in Constantinople. Thus his work contains many medical chapters of real value, and he gives one of the earliest accounts of recently discovered drugs and medicinal plants. Among other curiosities he maintained that he had discovered the Pygmies.

From this absorbing but confusing book our survey must turn finally to N.H. Wessely, who in 1782 for the first time maintained the importance of the study of geography in Jewish school education. The works of the past, with their consoling legends and hopes, continued to hold a place in the heart of Jewish readers. But from Wessely's time onwards a long series of Jewish explorers and travellers have joined the ranks of those who have opened up for modern times a real knowledge of the globe.

* * * * *

BIBLIOGRAPHY

Steinschneider.—*Jewish Literature*, p. 80.

A. Neubauer.—Series of Articles entitled *Where are the Ten Tribes*, *J.Q.R.*, Vol. I.

BENJAMIN OF TUDELA.

A. Asher.—*The Itinerary of Benjamin of Tudela* (with English translation and appendix by Zunz. London, 1840-1).

PETACHIAH OF RATISBON.

> A. Benisch.—*Travels of Petachia of Ratisbon* (with English translation. London, 1856).

ABRAHAM FARISSOL.

> Graetz.—IV, p. 413 [440].

DAVID REUBENI.

> Graetz.—IV, p. 491 [523].

H. WESSELY.

> Graetz.—V, p. 366 [388].

CHAPTER XXI

HISTORIANS AND CHRONICLERS

Order of the Tannaim and Amoraim.—Achimaaz.—Abraham Ibn Daud.—Josippon.—Historical Elegies, or Selichoth.—Memorial Books.—Abraham Zacuto.—Elijah Kapsali.—Usque.—Ibn Verga.—Joseph Cohen.—David Gans.—Gedaliah Ibn Yachya.—Azariah di Rossi.

The historical books to be found in the Bible, the Apocrypha, and the Hellenistic literature prove that the Hebrew genius was not unfitted for the presentation of the facts of Jewish life. These older works, as well as the writings of Josephus, also show a faculty for placing local records in relation to the wider facts of general history. After the dispersion of the Jews, however, the local was the only history in which the Jews could bear a part. The Jews read history as a mere commentary on their own fate, and hence they were unable to take the wide outlook into the world required for the compilation of objective histories. Thus, in their aim to find religious consolation for their sufferings in the Middle Ages, the Jewish historians sought rather to trace the hand of Providence than to analyze the human causes of the changes in the affairs of mankind.

But in another sense the Jews were essentially gifted with the historical spirit. The great men of Israel were not local heroes. Just as Plutarch's Lives were part of the history of the world's politics, so Jewish biographies of learned men were part of the history of the world's civilization. With the "Order of the Tannaim and Amoraim" (written about the year 1100) begins a series of such biographical works, in which more appreciation of sober fact is displayed than might have been expected from the period. In the same way the famous Letter of Sherira Gaon on the compilation of the Rabbinical literature (980) marked great progress in the critical examination of historical problems. Later works did not maintain the same level.

In the Middle Ages, Jewish histories mostly took the form of uncritical Chronicles, which included legends and traditions as well as assured facts. Their interest and importance lie in the personal and communal details with which they abound. Sometimes they are confessedly local. This is the case with the "Chronicle of Achimaaz," written by him in 1055 in rhymed prose. In an entertaining style, he tells of the early settlements of the Jews in Southern Italy, and throws much light on the intercommunication between the scattered Jewish congregations of his time. A larger canvas was filled by Abraham Ibn Daud, the physician and philosopher who was born in Toledo in 1110, and met a martyr's end at the age of seventy. His "Book of Tradition" (*Sefer ha-Kabbalah*), written in 1161, was designed to present, in opposition to the Karaites, the chain of Jewish tradition as a series of unbroken links from the age of Moses to Ibn Baud's own times. Starting with the Creation, his history ends with the anti-Karaitic crusade of Judah Ibn Ezra in Granada (1150). Abraham Ibn Daud shows in this work considerable critical power, but in his two other histories, one dealing with the history of Rome from its foundation to the time of King Reccared in Spain, the other a narrative of the history of the Jews during the Second Temple, the author relied entirely on "Josippon." This was a medieval concoction which long passed as the original Josephus. "Josippon" was a romance rather than a history. Culled from all sources, from Strabo, Lucian, and Eusebius, as well as from Josephus, this marvellous book exercised strong influence on the Jewish imagination, and supplied an antidote to the tribulations of the present by the consolations of the past and the vivid hopes for the future.

For a long period Abraham Ibn Daud found no imitators. Jewish history was written as part of the Jewish religion. Yet, incidentally, many historical passages were introduced in the works of Jewish scholars and travellers, and the liturgy was enriched by many beautiful historical Elegies, which were a constant call to heroism and fidelity. These Elegies, or *Selichoth*, were composed throughout the Middle Ages, and their passionate outpourings of lamentation and trust give them a high place in Jewish poetry. They are also important historically, and fully justify the fine utterance with which Zunz introduces them, an utterance which was translated by George Eliot as follows:

> If there are ranks in suffering, Israel takes precedence of all the nations—if the duration of sorrows and the patience with which they are borne ennoble, the Jews are among the aristocracy of every land—if a literature is called rich in the possession of a few classic tragedies, what shall we say to a National Tragedy lasting for fifteen hundred years, in which the poets and the actors were also the heroes?

The story of the medieval section of this pathetic martyrdom is written in the *Selichoth* and in the more prosaic records known as "Memorial Books" (in German, *Memorbücher*), which are lists of martyrs and brief eulogies of their careers.

For the next formal history we must pass to Abraham Zacuto. In his old age he employed some years of comparative quiet, after a stormy and unhappy life, in writing a "Book of Genealogies" (*Yuchasin*). He had been exiled from Spain in 1492, and twelve years later composed his historical work in Tunis. Like Abraham Ibn Baud's book, it opens with the Creation, and ends with the author's own day. Though Zacuto's work is more celebrated than historical, it nevertheless had an important share in reawaking the dormant interest of Jews in historical research. Thus we find Elijah Kapsali of Candia writing, in 1523, a "History of the Ottoman Empire," and Joseph Cohen, of Avignon, a "History of France and Turkey," in 1554, in which he included an account of the rebellion of Fiesco in Genoa, where the author was then residing.

The sixteenth century witnessed the production of several popular Jewish histories. At that epoch the horizon of the world was extending under new geographical and intellectual discoveries. Israel, on the other hand, seemed to be sinking deeper and deeper into the slough of despond. Some of the men who had themselves been the victims of persecution saw that the only hope lay in rousing the historical consciousness of their brethren. History became the consolation of the exiles from Spain who found themselves pent up within the walls of the Ghettos, which were first built in the sixteenth century. Samuel Usque was a fugitive from the Inquisition, and his dialogues, "Consolations for the Tribulations of Israel" (written in Portuguese, in 1553), are a long drawn-out sigh of pain passing into a sigh of relief. Usque opens with a passionate idyl in which the history of Israel in the near past is told by the shepherd Icabo. To him Numeo and Zicareo offer consolation, and they pour balm into his wounded heart. The vividness of Usque's style, his historical insight, his sturdy optimism, his poetical force in interpreting suffering as the means of attaining the highest life in God, raise his book above the other works of its class and age.

Usque's poem did not win the same popularity as two other elegiac histories of the same period. These were the "Rod of Judah" (*Shebet Jehudah*) and the "Valley of Tears" (*Emek ha-Bachah*). The former was the work of three generations of the Ibn Verga family. Judah died before the expulsion from Spain, but his son Solomon participated in the final troubles of the Spanish Jews, and was even forced to join the ranks of the Marranos. The grandson, Joseph Ibn Verga, became Rabbi in Adrianople, and was cultured in classical as well as Jewish lore. Their composite work, "The Rod of Judah," was completed in 1554. It is a well-written but badly arranged martyrology, and over all its pages might be inscribed the Talmudical motto, that God's chastisements of Israel are chastisements of love. The other work referred to is Joseph Cohen's "Valley of Tears," completed in 1575. The author was born in Avignon in 1496, four years after his father had shared in the exile from Spain. He himself suffered expatriation, for, though a distinguished physician and the private doctor of the Doge Andrea Doria, he was expelled with the rest of the Jews from Genoa in 1550. Settled in the little town of Voltaggio, he devoted himself to writing the annals of European and Jewish history. His style is clear and forcible, and recalls the lucid simplicity of the historical books of the Bible.

The only other histories that need be critically mentioned here are the "Branch of David" (*Zemach David*), the "Chain of Tradition" (*Shalsheleth ha-Kabbalah*), and the "Light of the Eyes" (*Meör Enayim*). Abraham de Porta Leone's "Shields of the Mighty"

(*Shilte ha-Gibborim*, printed in Mantua in 1612); Leon da Modena's "Ceremonies and Customs of the Jews," (printed in Paris in 1637); David Conforte's "Call of the Generations" (*Kore ha-Doroth*, written in Palestine in about 1670); Yechiel Heilprin's "Order of Generations" (*Seder ha-Doroth*, written in Poland in 1725); and Chayim Azulai's "Name of the Great Ones" (written in Leghorn in 1774), can receive only a bare mention.

The author of the "Branch of David," David Cans, was born in Westphalia in about 1540. He was the first German Jew of his age to take real interest in the study of history. He was a man of scientific culture, corresponded with Kepler, and was a personal friend of Tycho Brahe. For the latter Cans made a German translation of parts of the Hebrew version of the Tables of Alfonso, originally compiled in 1260. Cans wrote works on mathematical and physical geography, and treatises on arithmetic and geometry. His history, "Branch of David," was extremely popular. For a man of his scientific training it shows less critical power than might have been expected, but the German Jews did not begin to apply criticism to history till after the age of Mendelssohn. In one respect, however, the "Branch of David" displays the width of the author's culture. Not only does he tell the history of the Jews, but in the second part of his work he gives an account of many lands and cities, especially of Bohemia and Prague, and adds a striking description of the secret courts (*Vehmgerichte*) of Westphalia.

It is hard to think that the authors of the "Chain of Tradition" and of the "Light of the Eyes" were contemporaries. Azariah di Rossi (1514-1588), the writer of the last mentioned book, was the founder of historical criticism among the Jews. Elias del Medigo (1463-1498) had led in the direction, but di Rossi's work anticipated the methods, of the German school of "scientific" Jewish writers, who, at the beginning of the present century, applied scientific principles to the study of Jewish traditions. On the other hand, Gedaliah Ibn Yachya (1515-1587) was so utterly uncritical that his "Chain of Tradition" was nicknamed by Joseph Delmedigo the "Chain of Lies." Gedaliah was a man of wealth, and he expended his means in the acquisition of books and in making journeys in search of sacred and profane knowledge. Yet Gedaliah made up in style for his lack of historical method. The "Chain of Tradition" is a picturesque and enthralling book, it is a warm and cheery retrospect, and even deserves to be called a prose epic. Besides, many of his statements that were wont to be treated as altogether unauthentic have been vindicated by later research. Azariah di Rossi, on the other hand, is immortalized by his spirit rather than his actual contributions to historical literature. He came of an ancient family said to have been carried to Rome by Titus, and lived in Ferrara, where, in 1574, he produced his "Light of the Eyes." This is divided into three parts, the first devoted to general history, the second to the Letter of Aristeas, the third to the solution of several historical problems, all of which had been neglected by Jews and Christians alike. Azariah di Rossi was the first critic to open up true lines of research into the Hellenistic literature of the Jews of Alexandria. With him the true historical spirit once more descended on the Jewish genius.

* * * * *

BIBLIOGRAPHY

Steinschneider.—*Jewish Literature*, p. 75, *seq.*, 250 *seq.*
A. Neubauer.—Introductions to *Medieval Jewish Chronicles*, Vols. I and II (Oxford, 1882, etc.).

SELICHOTH.

Zunz.—*Sufferings of the Jews in the Middle Ages* (translated by A. Löwy, *Miscellany of the Society of Hebrew Literature*, Vol. I). See also *J.Q.R.*, VIII, pp. 78, 426, 611.

ABRAHAM IBN DAUD.

Graetz.—III, p. 363 [373].

ABRAHAM ZACUTO.

Graetz.—IV, pp. 366, 367, 391 [393].

ELIJAH KAPSALI.

Graetz.—IV, p. 406 [435].

JOSEPH COHEN, USQUE, IBN VERGA.

Graetz.—IV, p. 555 [590].

Chronicle of Joseph ben Joshua the Priest (English translation by Bialoblotzky. London, 1835-6).

ELIA DELMEDIGO.

Graetz.—IV, p. 290 [312].

DAVID GANS.

Graetz.—IV, p. 638 [679].

GEDALIAH IBN YACHYA.

Graetz.—IV, p. 609 [655].

AZARIAH DI ROSSI.

Graetz.—IV, p. 614 [653].

CHAPTER XXII

ISAAC ABARBANEL

Abarbanel's Philosophy and Biblical Commentaries.—Elias Levita.—Zeëna u-Reëna.—Moses Alshech.—The Biur.

The career of Don Isaac Abarbanel (born in Lisbon in 1437, died in Venice in 1509) worthily closes the long services which the Jews of Spain rendered to the state and to learning. The earlier part of his life was spent in the service of Alfonso V of Portugal. He possessed considerable wealth, and his house, which he himself tells us was built with spacious halls, was the meeting-place of scholars, diplomatists, and men of science. Among his other occupations, he busied himself in ransoming Jewish slaves, and obtained the co-operation of some Italian Jews in this object.

When Alfonso died, Abarbanel not only lost his post as finance minister, but was compelled to flee for his life. He shared the fall of the Duke of Braganza, whose popularity was hateful to Alfonso's successor. Don Isaac escaped to Castile in 1484, and, amid the friendly smiles of the cultured Jews of Toledo, set himself to resume the literary work he had been forced to lay aside while burdened with affairs of state. He began the compilation of commentaries on the historical books of the Bible, but he was not long left to his studies. Ferdinand and Isabella, under the very eyes of Torquemada and the Inquisition, entrusted the finances of their kingdom to the Jew Abarbanel during the years 1484 to 1492.

In the latter year, Abarbanel was driven from Spain in the general expulsion instigated by the Inquisition. He found a temporary asylum in Naples, where he also received a state appointment. But he was soon forced to flee again, this time to Corfu. "My wife, my sons, and my books are far from me," he wrote, "and I am left alone, a stranger in a strange land." But his spirit was not crushed by these successive misfortunes. He continued to compile huge works at a very rapid rate. He was not destined, however, to end his life in obscurity. In 1503 he was given a diplomatic post in Venice, and he passed his remaining years in happiness and honor. He ended the splendid roll of famous Spanish Jews with a career peculiarly Spanish. He gave a final, striking example of that association of life with literature which of old characterized Jews, but which found its greatest and last home in Spain.

As a writer, Abarbanel has many faults. He is very verbose, and his mannerisms are provoking. Thus, he always introduces his commentaries with a long string of questions, which he then proceeds to answer. It was jokingly said of him that he made many sceptics, for not one in a score of his readers ever got beyond the questions to the answers. There is this truth in the sarcasm, that Abarbanel, despite his essential lucidity, is very hard to read. Though Abarbanel has obvious faults, his good qualities are equally tangible. No predecessor of Abarbanel came so near as he did to the modern ideal of a commentator on the Bible. Ibn Ezra was the father of the "Higher Criticism," i.e. the attempt to explain the evolution of the text of Scripture. The Kimchis developed the strictly grammatical exposition of the Bible. But Abarbanel understood that, to explain the Bible, one must try to reproduce the atmosphere in which it was written; one must realize the ideas and the life of the times with which the narrative deals. His own practical state-craft stood him in good stead. He was able to form a conception of the politics of ancient Judea. His commentaries are works on the philosophy of history. His more formal philosophical works, such as his "Deeds of God" (*Miphaloth Elohim*), are of less value, they are borrowed in the main from Maimonides. In his Talmudical writings, notably his "Salvation of his Anointed" (*Yeshuoth Meshicho*), Abarbanel displays a lighter and more original touch than in his philosophical treatises. But his works on the Bible are his greatest literary achievement. Besides the merits already indicated, these books have another important excellence. He was the first Jew to make extensive use of Christian commentaries. He must be credited with the discovery that the study of the Bible may be unsectarian, and that all who hold the Bible in honor may join hands in elucidating it.

A younger contemporary of Abarbanel was also an apostle of the same view. This was Elias Levita (1469-1549). He was a Grammarian, or Massorite, i.e. a student of the tradition (*Massorah*) as to the Hebrew text of the Bible, and he was an energetic teacher of Christians. In the sixteenth century the study of Hebrew made much progress in Europe, but the Jews themselves were only indirectly associated with this advance. Despite Abarbanel, Jewish commentaries remained either homiletic or mystical, or, like the popular works of Moses Alshech, were more or less Midrashic in style. But the Bible was a real delight to the Jews, and it is natural that such books were often compiled for the masses. Mention must be made of the *Zeëna u-Reëna* ("Go forth and see"), a work written at the beginning of the eighteenth century in Jewish-German for the use of women, a work which is still beloved of the Jewess. But the seeds sown by Abarbanel and others of his school eventually produced an abundant harvest. Mendelssohn's German edition of the Pentateuch with the Hebrew Commentary (*Biur*) was the turning-point in the march towards the modern exposition of the Bible, which had been inaugurated by the statesman-scholar of Spain.

* * * * *

BIBLIOGRAPHY

BANEL.

    Graetz.—IV, II.
    I.S. Meisels.—*Don Isaac Abarbanel, J.Q.R.*, II, p. 37.
    S. Schechter.—*Studies in Judaism*, p. 173 [211].
    F.D. Mocatta.—*The Jews of Spain and Portugal and the Inquisition* (London, 1877).
    Schiller-Szinessy.—*Encycl. Brit.*, Vol. I, p. 52.

EXEGESIS 16TH-18TH CENTURIES.

    Steinschneider.—*Jewish Literature*, p. 232 *seq.*

BIUR.

    Specimen of the Biur, translated by A. Benisch (*Miscellany of the Society of Hebrew Literature*, Vol. I).

CHAPTER XXIII

THE SHULCHAN ARUCH

Asheri's Arba Turim.—Chiddushim and Teshuboth.—Solomon ben Adereth.—Meir of Rothenburg.—Sheshet and Duran.—Moses and Judah Minz.—Jacob Weil, Israel Isserlein, Maharil.—David Abi Zimra.—Joseph Karo.—Jair Bacharach.—Chacham Zevi.—Jacob Emden.—Ezekiel Landau.

The religious literature of the Jews, so far as practical life was concerned, culminated in the publication of the "Table Prepared" (*Shulchan Aruch*), in 1565. The first book of its kind compiled after the invention of printing, the Shulchan Aruch obtained a popularity denied to all previous works designed to present a digest of Jewish ethics and ritual observances. It in no sense superseded the "Strong Hand" of Maimonides, but it was so much more practical in its scope, so much clearer as a work of general reference, so much fuller of *Minhag*, or established custom, that it speedily became the universal hand-book of Jewish life in many of its phases. It was not accepted in all its parts, and its blemishes were clearly perceived. The author, Joseph Karo, was too tender to the past, and admitted some things which had a historical justification, but which Karo himself would have been the first to reject as principles of conduct for his own or later times. On the whole, the book was a worthy summary of the fundamental Jewish view, that religion is co-extensive with life, and that everything worth doing at all ought to be done in accordance with a general principle of obedience to the divine will. The defects of such a view are the defects of its qualities.

The Shulchan Aruch was the outcome of centuries of scholarship. It was original, yet it was completely based on previous works. In particular the "Four Rows" (*Arbäa Turim*) of Jacob Asheri (1283-1340) was one of the main sources of Karo's work. The "Four Rows," again, owed everything to Jacob's father, Asher, the son of Yechiel, who migrated from Germany to Toledo at the very beginning of the fourteenth century. But besides the systematic codes of his predecessors, Karo was able to draw on a vast mass of literature on the Talmud and on Jewish Law, accumulated in the course of centuries.

There was, in the first place, a large collection of "Novelties" (*Chiddushim*), or Notes on the Talmud, by various authorities. More significant, however, were the "Responses" (*Teshuboth*), which resembled those of the Gaonim referred to in an earlier chapter. The Rabbinical Correspondence, in the form of Responses to Questions sent from far and near, covered the whole field of secular and religious knowledge. The style of these "Responses" was at first simple, terse, and full of actuality. The most famous representatives of this form of literature after the Gaonim were both of the thirteenth century, Solomon, the son of Adereth, in Spain, and Meir of Rothenburg in Germany. Solomon, the son of Adereth, of Barcelona, was a man whose moral earnestness, mild yet firm disposition, profound erudition, and tolerant character, won for him a supreme place in Jewish life for half a century. Meir of Rothenburg was a poet and martyr as well as a profound scholar. He passed many years in prison rather than yield to the rapacious demands of the local government for a ransom, which Meir's friends would willingly have paid. As a specimen of Meir's poetry, the following verses are taken from a dirge composed by him in 1285, when copies of the Pentateuch were publicly committed to the flames. The "Law" is addressed in the second person:

> Dismay hath seized upon my soul; how then
> Can food be sweet to me?
> When, O thou Law! I have beheld base men
> Destroying thee?
>
> Ah! sweet 'twould be unto mine eyes alway
> Waters of tears to pour,

To sob and drench thy sacred robes, till they
Could hold no more.

But lo! my tears are dried, when, fast outpoured,
They down my cheeks are shed,
Scorched by the fire within, because thy Lord
Hath turned and sped.

Yea, I am desolate and sore bereft,
Lo! a forsaken one,
Like a sole beacon on a mountain left,
A tower alone.

I hear the voice of singers now no more,
Silence their song hath bound,
For broken are the strings on harps of yore,
Viols of sweet sound.

I am astonied that the day's fair light
Yet shineth brilliantly
On all things; but is ever dark as night
To me and thee.

* * * * *

Even as when thy Rock afflicted thee,
He will assuage thy woe,
And turn again the tribes' captivity,
And raise the low.

Yet shalt thou wear thy scarlet raiment choice,
And sound the timbrels high,
And glad amid the dancers shalt rejoice,
With joyful cry.

My heart shall be uplifted on the day
Thy Rock shall be thy light,
When he shall make thy gloom to pass away,
Thy darkness bright.

This combination of the poetical with the legal mind was parallelled by other combinations in such masters of "Responses" as the Sheshet and Duran families in Algiers in the fourteenth and fifteenth centuries. In these men depth of learning was associated with width of culture. Others, such as Moses and Judah Minz, Jacob Weil, and Israel Isserlein, whose influence was paramount in Germany in the fifteenth century, were less cultivated, but their learning was associated with a geniality and sense of humor that make their "Responses" very human and very entertaining. There is the same homely, affectionate air in the collection of *Minhagim*, or Customs, known as the *Maharil*, which belongs to the same period. On the other hand, David Abi Zimra, Rabbi of Cairo in the sixteenth century, was as independent as he was learned. It was he, for instance, who abolished the old custom of dating Hebrew documents from the Seleucid era (311 B.C.E.). And, to pass beyond the time of Karo, the writers of "Responses" include the gifted Jair Chayim Bacharach (seventeenth century), a critic as well as a legalist; Chacham Zevi and Jacob Emden in Amsterdam, and Ezekiel Landau in Prague, the former two of whom opposed the Messianic claims of Sabbatai Zevi, and the last of whom was an antagonist to the Germanizing tendency of Moses Mendelssohn.

Joseph Karo himself was a man of many parts. He was born in Spain in 1488, and died in Safed, the nest of mysticism, in 1575. Master of the Talmudic writings of his predecessors from his youth, Karo devoted thirty-two years to the preparation of an exhaustive commentary on the "Four Rows" of Jacob Asheri. This occupied him from 1522 to 1554. Karo was an enthusiast as well as a student, and the emotional side of the Kabbala had much fascination for him. He believed that he had a familiar, or *Maggid*, the personification of the Mishnah, who appeared to him in dreams, and held communion with him. He found a congenial home in Safed, where the mystics had their head-quarters in the sixteenth century. Karo's companion on his journey to Safed was Solomon Alkabets, author of the famous Sabbath hymn "Come, my Friend" (*Lecha Dodi*), with the refrain:

> Come forth, my friend, the Bride to meet,
> Come, O my friend, the Sabbath greet!

The Shulchan Aruch is arranged in four parts, called fancifully, "Path of Life" (*Orach Chayim*), "Teacher of Knowledge" (*Yoreh Deah*), "Breastplate of Judgment" (*Choshen ha-Mishpat*), and "Stone of Help" (*Eben ha-Ezer*). The first part is mainly occupied with the subject of prayer, benedictions, the Sabbath, the festivals, and the observances proper to each. The second part deals with food and its preparation, *Shechitah*, or slaughtering of animals for food, the relations between Jews and non-Jews, vows, respect to parents, charity, and religious observances connected with agriculture, such as the payment of tithes, and, finally, the rites of mourning. This section of the Shulchan Aruch is the most miscellaneous of the four; in the other three the association of subjects is more logical. The Eben ha-Ezer treats of the laws of marriage and divorce from their civil and religious aspects. The Choshen ha-Mishpat deals with legal procedure, the laws regulating business transactions and the relations between man and man in the conduct of worldly affairs. A great number of commentaries on Karo's Code were written by and for the *Acharonim* (=later scholars). It fully deserved this attention, for on its own lines the Shulchan Aruch was a masterly production. It brought system into the discordant opinions of the Rabbinical authorities of the Middle Ages, and its publication in the sixteenth century was itself a stroke of genius. Never before had such a work been so necessary as then. The Jews were in sight of what was to them the darkest age, the seventeenth and eighteenth centuries. Though the Shulchan Aruch had an evil effect in stereotyping Jewish religious thought and in preventing the rapid spread of the critical spirit, yet it was a rallying point for the disorganized Jews, and saved them from the disintegration which threatened them. The Shulchan Aruch was the last great bulwark of the Rabbinical conception of life. Alike in its form and contents it was a not unworthy close to the series of codes which began with the Mishnah, and in which life itself was codified.

* * * * *

BIBLIOGRAPHY

Steinschneider.—*Jewish Literature*, p. 213 *seq.*
I.H. Weiss.—On *Codes, J.Q.R.*, I, p. 289.

ASHER BEN YECHIEL.

Graetz.—IV, p. 34 [37].

JACOB ASHERI.

Graetz.—IV, p. 88 [95].

SOLOMON BEN ADERETH.

Graetz.—III, p. 618 [639].

MEIR OF ROTHENBURG.

Graetz.—III, pp. 625, 638 [646].

JUDAH MINZ.

Graetz.—IV, p. 294 [317].

MAHARIL.

S. Schechter.—*Studies in Judaism*, p. 142 [173].

DAVID BEN ABI ZIMRA.

Graetz.—IV, p. 393 [420].

JAIR CHAYIM BACHARACH.

D. Kaufmann, *J.Q.R.*, III, p. 292, etc.

JOSEPH KARO.

Graetz.—IV, p. 537 [571].

MOSES ISSERLES.

Graetz.—IV, p. 637 [677].

CHIDDUSHIM.

Graetz.—IV, p. 641 [682].

CHAPTER XXIV

AMSTERDAM IN THE
SEVENTEENTH CENTURY

Manasseh ben Israel.—Baruch Spinoza.—The Drama in Hebrew.—
Moses Zacut, Joseph Felix Penso, Moses Chayim Luzzatto.

Holland was the centre of Jewish hope in the seventeenth
century, and among its tolerant and cultivated people the Marranos,
exiled from Spain and Portugal, founded a new Jerusalem. Two
writers of Marrano origin, wide as the poles asunder in gifts of
mind and character, represented two aspects of the aspiration of
the Jews towards a place in the wider world. Manasseh ben Israel
(1604-1657) was an enthusiast who based his ambitious hopes
on the Messianic prophecies; Baruch Spinoza (1632-1677) lacked
enthusiasm, had little belief in the verbal promises of Scripture,
yet developed a system of ethics in which God filled the world.
Manasseh ben Israel regained for the Jews admission to England;
Spinoza reclaimed the right of a Jew to a voice in the philosophy of
the world. Both were political thinkers who maintained the full rights
of the individual conscience, and though the arguments used vary
considerably, yet Manasseh ben Israel's splendid *Vindiciæ Judeorum*
and Spinoza's "Tractate" alike insist on the natural right of men to
think freely. They anticipated some of the greatest principles that
won acceptance at the end of the eighteenth century.

Manasseh ben Israel was born in Lisbon of Marrano parents,
who emigrated to Amsterdam a few years after their son's birth. He
displayed a youthful talent for oratory, and was a noted preacher
in his teens. He started the first Hebrew printing-press established

in Amsterdam, and from it issued many works still remarkable for the excellence of their type and general workmanship. Manasseh was himself, not only a distinguished linguist, but a popularizer of linguistic studies. He wrote well in Hebrew, Latin, English, Spanish, and Portuguese, and was the means of instructing many famous Christians of the day in Hebrew and Rabbinic. Among his personal friends were Vossius, who translated Manasseh's "Conciliator" from Spanish into Latin. This, the most important of Manasseh's early writings, was as popular with Christians as with Jews, for it attempted to reconcile the discrepancies and contradictions apparent in the Bible. Another of his friends was the painter Rembrandt, who, in 1636, etched the portrait of Manasseh. Huet and Grotius were also among the friends and disciples who gathered round the Amsterdam Rabbi.

An unexpected result of Manasseh ben Israel's zeal for the promotion of Hebrew studies among his own brethren was the rise of a new form of poetical literature. The first dramas in Hebrew belong to this period. Moses Zacut and Joseph Felix Penso wrote Hebrew dramas in the first half of the seventeenth century in Amsterdam. The "Foundation of the World" by the former and the "Captives of Hope" by the latter possess little poetical merit, but they are interesting signs of the desire of Jews to use Hebrew for all forms of literary art. Hence these dramas were hailed as tokens of Jewish revival. Strangely enough, the only great writer of Hebrew plays, Moses Chayim Luzzatto (1707-1747), was also resident in Amsterdam. Luzzatto wrote under the influence of the Italian poet Guarini. His metres, his long soliloquies, his lyrics, his dovetailing of rural and urban scenery, are all directly traceable to Guarini. Luzzatto was nevertheless an original poet. His mastery of Hebrew was complete, and his rich fancy was expressed in glowing lines. His dramas, "Samson," the "Strong Tower," and "Glory to the Virtuous," show classical refinement and freshness of touch, which have made them the models of all subsequent efforts of Hebrew dramatists.

Manasseh ben Israel did not allow himself to become absorbed in the wider interests opened out to him by his intimacy with the greatest Christian scholars of his day. He prepared a Spanish translation of the Pentateuch for the Amsterdam Jews, who were slow to adopt Dutch as their speech, a fact not wonderful when it is remembered that literary Dutch was only then forming. Manasseh also wrote at this period a Hebrew treatise on immortality. His worldly prosperity was small, and he even thought of emigrating to Brazil. But the friends of the scholar found a post for him in a new college for the study of Hebrew, a college to which it is probable that Spinoza betook himself. In the meantime the reports of Montesinos as to the presence of the Lost Ten Tribes in America turned the current of Manasseh's life. In 1650 he wrote his famous essay, the "Hope of Israel," which he dedicated to the English Parliament. He argued that, as a preliminary to the restoration of Israel, or the millennium, for which the English Puritans were eagerly looking, the dispersion of Israel must be complete. The hopes of the millennium were doomed to disappointment unless the Jews were readmitted to England, "the isle of the Northern Sea." His dedication met with a friendly reception, Manasseh set out for England in 1655, and obtained from Cromwell a qualified consent to the resettlement of the Jews in the land from which they had been expelled in 1290.

The pamphlets which Manasseh published in England deserve a high place in literature and in the history of modern thought. They are immeasurably superior to his other works, which are eloquent but diffuse, learned but involved. But in his *Vindiciæ Judeorum* (1656) his style and thought are clear, original, elevated. There are here no mystic irrelevancies. His remarks are to the point, sweetly reasonable, forcible, moderate. He grapples with the medieval prejudices against the Jews in a manner which places his works among the best political pamphlets ever written. Morally, too, his manner is noteworthy. He pleads for Judaism in a spirit equally removed from arrogance and self-abasement. He is dignified in his persuasiveness. He appeals to a sense of justice rather than mercy, yet he writes as one who knows that justice is the rarest and highest quality of human nature; as one who knows that humbly to express gratitude for justice received is to do reverence to the noblest faculty of man.

Fate rather than disposition tore Manasseh from his study to plead before the English Parliament. Baruch Spinoza was spared such distraction. Into his self-contained life the affairs of the world could effect no entry. It is not quite certain whether Spinoza was born in Amsterdam. He must, at all events, have come there in his early youth. He may have been a pupil of Manasseh, but his mind was nurtured on the philosophical treatises of Maimonides and Crescas. His thought became sceptical, and though he was "intoxicated with a sense of God," he had no love for any positive religion. He learned Latin, and found new avenues opened to him in the writings of Descartes. His associations with the representatives of the Cartesian philosophy and his own indifference to ceremonial observances brought him into collision with the Synagogue, and, in 1656, during the absence of Manasseh in England, Spinoza was excommunicated by the Amsterdam Rabbis. Spinoza was too strong to seek the weak revenge of an abjuration of Judaism. He went on quietly earning a living as a maker of lenses; he refused a professorship, preferring, like Maimonides before him, to rely on other than literary pursuits as a means of livelihood.

In 1670 Spinoza finished his "Theologico-Political Tractate," in which some bitterness against the Synagogue is apparent. His attack on the Bible is crude, but the fundamental principles of modern criticism are here anticipated. The main importance of the "Tractate" lay in the doctrine that the state has full rights over the individual, except in relation to freedom of thought and free expression of thought. These are rights which no human being can alienate to the state. Of Spinoza's greatest work, the "Ethics," it need only be said that it was one of the most stimulating works of modern times. A child of Judaism and of Cartesianism, Spinoza won a front place among the great teachers of mankind.

* * * * *

BIBLIOGRAPHY

MANASSEH BEN ISRAEL.

Graetz.—V, 2.
H. Adler.—*Transactions of the Jewish Historical Society of England*, Vol. I, p. 25.
Kayserling.—*Miscellany of the Society of Hebrew Literature*, Vol. I.
Lady Magnus.—*Jewish Portraits*, p. 109.

English translations of works, *Vindiciæ Judeorum, Hope of Israel, The Conciliator* (E.H. Lindo, 1841, etc.).

SPINOZA.

Graetz.—V, 4.

J. Freudenthal.—*History of Spinozism, J.Q.R.*, VIII, p. 17.

HEBREW DRAMAS.

Karpeles.—*Jewish Literature and other Essays*, p. 229.

Abrahams.—*Jewish Life in the Middle Ages*, ch. 14.

Graetz,—V, pp, 112 [119], 234 [247].

CHAPTER XXV

MOSES MENDELSSOHN

Mendelssohn's German Translation of the Bible.—Phædo.—
Jerusalem.—Lessing's "Nathan the Wise."

Moses, the son of Mendel, was born in Dessau in 1728, and
died in Berlin in 1786. His father was poor, and he himself was
of a weak constitution. But his stunted form was animated by a
strenuous spirit. After a boyhood passed under conditions which
did little to stimulate his dawning aspirations, Mendelssohn resolved
to follow his teacher Fränkel to Berlin. He trudged the whole way
on foot, and was all but refused admission into the Prussian capital,
where he was destined to produce so profound an impression. In
Berlin his struggle with poverty continued, but his condition was
improved when he obtained a post, first as private tutor, then as
book-keeper in a silk factory.

Berlin was at this time the scene of an intellectual and æsthetic
revival dominated by Frederick the Great. The latter, a dilettante in
culture, was, as Mendelssohn said of him, a man "who made the
arts and sciences flourish, and made liberty of thought universal
in his realm." The German Jews were as yet outside this revival.
In Italy and Holland the new movements of the seventeenth and
the eighteenth century had found Jews well to the fore. But the
"German" Jews—and this term included the great bulk of the
Jews of Europe—were suffering from the effects of intellectual
stagnation. The Talmud still exercised the mind and imagination of
these Jews, but culture and religion were separated. Mendelssohn
in a hundred places contends that such separation is dangerous and

unnatural. It was his service to Judaism that he made the separation once for all obsolete.

Mendelssohn effected this by purely literary means. Most reformations have been at least aided by moral and political forces. But the Mendelssohnian revival in Judaism was a literary revival, in which moral and religious forces had only an indirect influence. By the aid of greater refinement of language, for hitherto the "German" Jews had not spoken pure German; by a widening of the scope of education in the Jewish schools; by the introduction of all that is known as culture, Mendelssohn changed the whole aspect of Jewish life. And he produced this reformation by books and by books alone. Never playing the part of a religious or moral reformer, Mendelssohn became the Jewish apostle of culture.

The great event of his life occurred in 1754, when he made the acquaintance of Lessing. The two young men became constant friends. Lessing, before he knew Mendelssohn, had written a drama, "The Jews," in which, perhaps for the first time, a Jew was represented on the stage as a man of honor. In Mendelssohn, Lessing recognized a new Spinoza; in Lessing, Mendelssohn saw the perfect ideal of culture. The masterpiece of Lessing's art, the drama "Nathan the Wise," was the monument of this friendship. Mendelssohn was the hero of the drama, and the toleration which it breathes is clearly Mendelssohn's. Mendelssohn held that there was no absolutely best religion any more than there was an absolutely best form of government. This was the leading idea of his last work, "Jerusalem"; it is also the central thought of "Nathan the Wise." The best religion, according to both, is the religion which best brings out the individual's noblest faculties. As Mendelssohn wrote, there are certain eternal truths which God implants in all men alike, but "Judaism boasts of no exclusive revelation of immutable truths indispensable to salvation." *unique revelation to Israel and mankind*

What has just been quoted is one of the last utterances of Mendelssohn. We must retrace our steps to the date of his first intimacy with Lessing. He devoted his attention to the perfecting of his German style, and succeeded so well that his writings have gained a place among the classics of German literature. In 1763, he won the Berlin prize for an essay on Mathematical Method in Philosophical Reasoning, and defeated Kant entirely on account of his lucid and attractive style. Mendelssohn's most popular philosophical work, "Phædo, or the Immortality of the Soul," won extraordinary popularity in Berlin, as much for its attractive form as for its spiritual charms. The "German Plato," the "Jewish Socrates," were some of the epithets bestowed on him by multitudes of admirers. Indeed, the "Phædo" of Mendelssohn is a work of rare beauty.

One of the results of Mendelssohn's popularity was a curious correspondence with Lavater. The latter perceived in Mendelssohn's toleration signs of weakness, and believed that he could convert the famous Jew to Christianity. Mendelssohn's reply, like his "Jerusalem" and his admirable preface to a German translation of Manasseh ben Israel's *Vindiciæ Judeorum*, gave voice to that claim on personal liberty of thought and conscience for which the Jews, unconsciously, had been so long contending. Mendelssohn's view was that all true religious aspirations are independent of religious forms. Mendelssohn did not ignore the value of forms, but he held that as there are often several means to the same end, so the various religious forms of the various creeds may all lead their respective adherents to salvation and to God.

Mendelssohn's most epoch-making work was his translation of the Pentateuch into German. With this work the present history finds a natural close. Mendelssohn's Pentateuch marks the modernization of the literature of Judaism. There was much opposition to the book, but on the other hand many Jews eagerly scanned its pages, acquired its noble diction, and committed its rhythmic eloquence to their hearts. Round Mendelssohn there clustered a band of devoted disciples, the pioneers of the new learning, the promoters of a literature of Judaism, in which the modern spirit reanimated the still living records of antiquity. There was certainly some weakness among the men and women affected by the Berlin philosopher, for some discarded all positive religion, because the master had taught that all positive religions had their saving and truthful elements.

It is not, however, the province of this sketch to trace the religious effects of the Mendelssohnian movement. Suffice it to say that, while the old Jewish conception had been that literature and life are co-extensive, Jewish literature begins with Mendelssohn to have an independent life of its own, a life of the spirit, which cannot be altogether controlled by the tribulations of material life. A physical Ghetto may once more be imposed on the Jews from without; an intellectual Ghetto imposed from within is hardly conceivable. Tolerance gave the modern spirit to Jewish literature, but intolerance cannot withdraw it.

* * * * *

BIBLIOGRAPHY

MOSES MENDELSSOHN.

Graetz.—V, 8.

Karpeles.—*Sketch of Jewish History*, p. 93; *Jewish Literature and other Essays*, p. 293.

English translations of *Phædo, Jerusalem,* and of the *Introduction to the Pentateuch* (*Hebrew Review*, Vol. I).

Other translations of *Jerusalem* were made by M. Samuels (London, 1838) and by Isaac Leeser, the latter published as a supplement to the *Occident*, Philadelphia, 5612.

MENDELSSOHNIAN MOVEMENT.

Graetz.—V, 10.

BIBLIOBAZAAR

The essential book market!

Did you know that you can get any of our titles in large print?

Did you know that we have an ever-growing collection of books in many languages?

Order online:
www.bibliobazaar.com

Find all of your favorite classic books!

Stay up to date with the latest government reports!

At BiblioBazaar, we aim to make knowledge more accessible by making thousands of titles available to you- *quickly and affordably*.

Contact us:
BiblioBazaar
PO Box 21206
Charleston, SC 29413

List of authors !

LaVergne, TN USA
22 October 2010
201848LV00001B/64/A